COMMUNITIES OF PEACE

VALUE INQUIRY BOOK SERIES

VIBS

Volume 229

a volume in
Philosophy of Peace
POP
William C. Gay, Editor

COMMUNITIES OF PEACE
Confronting Injustice and Creating Justice

Edited by

Danielle Poe

Rodopi

Amsterdam - New York, NY 2011

Cover Photo: www.Morguefile.com

Cover Design: Studio Pollmann

The paper on which this book is printed meets the requirements of "ISO 9706:1994, Information and documentation - Paper for documents - Requirements for permanence".

ISBN: 978-90-420-3335-1
E-Book ISBN: 978-94-012-0035-6
© Editions Rodopi B.V., Amsterdam - New York, NY 2011
Printed in the Netherlands

Philosophy of Peace
(POP)

William C. Gay
Editor

Other Titles in POP

Laurence F. Bove and Laura Duhan Kaplan, eds. *From the Eye of the Storm: Regional Conflicts and the Philosophy of Peace.* 1995. VIBS 29

Laura Duhan Kaplan and Laurence F. Bove, eds. *Philosophical Perspectives on Power and Domination: Theories and Practices.* 1997. VIBS 49

HPP (Hennie) Lötter. *Injustice, Violence, and Peace: The Case of South Africa.* 1997. VIBS 56

Deane Curtin and Robert Litke, eds. *Institutional Violence.* 1999. VIBS 88

Judith Presler and Sally J. Scholz, eds. *Peacemaking: Lessons from the Past, Visions for the Future.* 2000. VIBS 105

Alison Bailey and Paula J. Smithka, eds. *Community, Diversity, and Difference: Implications for Peace.* 2002. VIBS 127

Nancy Nyquist Potter, ed. *Putting Peace into Practice: Evaluating Policy on Local and Global Levels.* 2004. VIBS 164

John Kultgen and Mary Lenzi, eds. *Problems for Democracy.* 2006. VIBS 181

David Boersema and Katy Gray Brown, eds. *Spiritual and Political Dimensions of Nonviolence and Peace.* 2006. VIBS 182

Gail Presbey, ed., *Philosophical Perspectives on the "War on Terrorism.* 2007. VIBS 188

Danielle Poe and Eddy Souffrant, eds., *Parceling the Globe: Explorations in Globalization, Global Behavior, and Peace.* 2008. VIBS 194

Carmen R. Lugo-Lugo and Mary K. Bloodworth-Lugo, eds. *A New Kind of Containment: "The War on Terror," Race, and Sexuality.* 2009. VIBS 201

Andrew Fitz-Gibbon. *Positive Peace: Reflections on Peace Education, Non-violence, and Social Change.* 2010. VIBS 217

Mary K. Bloodsworth-Lugo and Carmen R. Lugo-Lugo. *Containing (Un)American Bodies: Race, Sensuality, and Post-9/11 Constructions of Citizenship.* 2010. VIBS 219

Rob Gildert and Dennis Rothermel, eds. *Remembrance and Reconciliation.* 2011. VIBS 225

Assistant Editor of POP
Danielle Poe

CONTENTS

COMMUNITIES OF PEACE

EDITORIAL FOREWORD

This volume is the sixteenth one to appear in the Philosophy of Peace Special Series since its inception in 1995. The fact that this Special Series is averaging the publication of one book per year since that time is testament to the growing academic importance of the Philosophy of Peace and to the emergence of a mutigenerational scholarly community committed to advancing the field.

Only a few volumes in this Special Series have focused specifically on issues of community. *Community, Diversity, and Difference: Implications for Peace* (VIBS 127, 2000), edited by Alison Bailey and Paula J. Smithka, addressed themes of difference and community and the ideal of global community. *Positive Peace: Reflections on Peace Education, Nonviolence, and Social Change* (VIBS 217, 2010), edited by Andrew Fitz-Gibbon, focuses on the requirements for positive peace which is an essential component for just communities. Danielle Poe, the editor of the present volume titled *Communities of Peace: Confronting Injustice and Creating Justice*, extends these efforts by bringing together eight essays that explore various facets of the quest for just communities.

Several of the authors (William C. Gay, Tanya Loughead, and Fitz-Gibbon) address specific needs for and in a just community, and I note a few of their suggestions. Biological diversity is needed in ecological communities, and cultural diversity is needed in human communities. The desire for a just community needs to be cultivated, and love can play an important role in constructing a just community.

Other authors (Wendy C. Hamblet, Arnold L. Farr, Matthew Pianalto, Courtland Lewis, and V. Denise James) address techniques and methods for addressing structures and practices of injustice that continue during the quest for just communities. Among the techniques and methods proposed, I shall mention a few of the most significant ones. Efforts need to be made to find just methods for responding to unjust behavior. Responses need to be developed that address residual systems of privilege, and means need to be found to identify and assist the least advantaged in a community. In order to maintain just communities ways need to be found for tolerating remaining differences. Furthermore, methods need to be found for transforming negative emotions into active nonviolent responses.

Taken together, these essays provide an indication of the many challenges to be faced in seeking to create and then to maintain just communities. At the same time, these essays also provide ground breaking proposals for seeking to create just communities and for addressing residual unjust structures and practices. These contributors provide the basis for further theoretical reflection and practical action.

Achievement of just communities involves formidable challenges, but these authors give us hope that such efforts need not be viewed as quixotic.

To paraphrase Immanuel Kant, because the achievement of just communities is possible, we have a moral duty to seek to advance them.

The present volume provides a set of essays by authors who recognize the possibility of creating just communities and who also take on this moral responsibility. As a result of these efforts, this volume provides us with concrete steps on the journey to the creation of just communities and extends to us an invitation to take further steps. For these reasons, this volume is a very welcome addition to the Philosophy of Peace Special Series.

William C. Gay, Professor of Philosophy
University of North Carolina at Charlotte
Philosophy of Peace Special Series Editor

PREFACE

For more than twenty-two years, philosophers from around the world have come together at Concerned Philosophers for Peace conferences to discuss what peace means, the obstacles to peace, and means to overcome these obstacles. These conferences bring together philosophers with a wide range of subspecialties from philosophy of law to environmental ethics, but they bring that expertise together to think about how the world can be a better place. This volume brings together contributions that were selected from the annual conference at the University of Dayton in 2009 where the theme was *Communities of Justice*.

At this conference, philosophers focused on what a just community is and how to create a just community in particular contexts. Participants were, then, invited to submit papers for blind review and consideration for this volume. The contributors focus on some of the most pressing obstacles to peace including violence, oppression, and current forms of punishment. They also suggest ways to utilize resources within communities to move toward peace.

Danielle Poe, Associate Professor of Philosophy
University of Dayton

INTRODUCTION

Danielle Poe

William C. Gay opens this volume with an analysis of what kind of community is desirable. In "Community and Diversity," Gay draws on the work of Charles Darwin to demonstrate that diversity is a necessary feature of ecological communities.Gay's work leads to a critique of human attempts to restrict diversity through domination and militarism. In conclusion, Gay uses this analysis of diversity, domination, and militarism to demonstrate that diversity is desirable and a necessary feature of a just community.

Every community must have some method of addressing wrongdoing, but a just community must find some way to do so that promotes peace. Wendy C. Hamblet, in "From the Scaffold to Prison to the Nursery: The Shame of Punishment," analyzes current punishment practices to reveal their failure to correct wrongdoing. Her critical analysis reveals that contemporary practices are not the only way that wrongdoing could be addressed. By showing the deficiency of current methods, Hamblet opens the possibility for new, just ways to correct people's unjust behavior.

Arnold L. Farr also addresses the theme of identifying and correcting wrongs to create a just community. In his chapter, "Repressive Justice: Marcuse, Adorno, and the American Attempt to Live Wrong Life Rightly," Farr critiques habits and values that serve to uphold a system of privilege for the elite at the expense of everyone else. To correct the injustices of systems of privilege for the elite, he concludes that we must turn to a liberation philosophy; he holds that those who have the greatest disadvantages should be privileged. Farr's conclusion that, in a just society, the least advantaged ought to be privileged raises a question about how we can determine who the least advantaged are.

Andrew Fitz-Gibbon's chapter, "Intersectionality and Love" helps us think about the ways in which people can be part of an intersection between being oppressed and oppressing others. From his description of intersectionality, Fitz-Gibbon addresses how understanding it leads to moral directives. Specifically, love can guide our responses to overcome oppression.

With Fitz-Gibbon and Gay, who describe just communities as communities that embrace difference, Matthew Pianalto agrees that a just community embraces difference. However, he confronts the reality of living in a society where differences are more than a variety of preferences that coexist easily. Sometimes differences can place moral convictions and personal integrity in conflict. In "Moral Conviction and Disagreement: Getting beyond Negative Toleration," Pianalto argues that even when individuals come into conflict because of their moral convictions, we can tolerate difference and live together peacefully.

V. Denise James takes on the challenge of finding ways to live together peacefully in "In Support of the Girls from 'Round Here: Black Feminist Reflections on the Utility of Rage for Building Communities of Support." James begins with concrete observations about the rage she feels when she witnesses young, black boys verbally assaulting a young, black girl. Rather than trying to move to an abstract level where rage is irrelevant, James uses that anger and rage to propose ways in which domination and violence can be resisted. Thus, emotions that, in other contexts, lead to violence, are transformed into forces for active non-violent resistance that allow the community to become a better place.

Court Lewis builds on the theme of addressing a world that is filled with violence and domination. In his chapter, "A Sketch of the Moral Responsibility to Engage One's Oppressor," Lewis examines the ways in which people who are oppressed can engage their oppressors and agitate for improved conditions in society. Lewis recognizes that depending on the kind of oppression suffered, different responses will be appropriate. In some cases, face-to-face engagement with one's oppressor leads to more just conditions; in other cases, indirect engagement engages the oppressor, but keeps the victim from being further harmed. According to Lewis, victims should find appropriate ways to engage their oppressors in order to overcome that oppression and to help create a just society.

The final chapter in this volume, "The Radical Praxis of Teaching for a Just Community: Marcuse and Kristeva on Liberating the Subject," Tanya Loughead suggests practical ways that those who teach can confront injustice to help create a just society. Loughead argues that, when we consider the challenges of creating a just community, we must also consider how to cultivate in ourselves and others the desire to create a just community. Through psychoanalysis and Marxist theory, Loughead suggests a model for radical teaching that would nourish this desire for transformation.

As a whole, this volume examines the many ways in which violence, domination, and oppression manifest themselves. This examination opens the way to creative suggestions for overcoming injustice. The authors in this volume also describe the features of a just community and inspire readers to implement peaceful transformation.

One

COMMUNITY AND DIVERSITY

William C. Gay

1. Introduction

Throughout the history of social and political thought, theorists have addressed the issue of how to define community. From the time of Plato through the work of John Rawls, these discussions have often been linked to considerations of justice (Plato, 1941; Rawls, 1999). Recently, efforts have been made to include issues of biological and cultural diversity into discussion of what constitutes just communities (Gay, 2002). In addition, the connection of militarism to threats to biological and cultural diversity has received increased attention (Klare, 1980, p. 37).

In this chapter, I will support the view that community needs diversity and that just communities require biological and cultural diversity. I will trace a model for how communities are restructured and how such restructuring can be negative or positive, though historically, negative reconstruction has prevailed. Finally, I will suggest that, for global justice, we also need to welcome diversity in the geopolitical relations among communities.

2. The Social Reconstruction of Cultures

In *The Origin of Species*, Charles Darwin documented that over relatively brief periods of time we see biological variation resulting from the cultivation of plants and the domestication of animals (1962, pp. 47–49). Using the scale of time suggested by Charles Lyell's 1830, *The Principles of Geology* (1997), and the struggle for survival suggested by Thomas Malthus's 1798, *An Essay on Population* (1914), Darwin argued for the evolution of the species.

Ironically, the principle of biological evolution is much more conservative than the practice of cultural revolution that Darwin unwittingly uncovered (Lyell, 1997; Malthus, 1914). While the consequences of unconscious and random biological evolution span millennia, the consequences of intentional and planned cultural revolution occur over mere decades. In a very real sense, the early chapters of *The Origin of Species* support a far more radical thesis than Darwin realized.

If we extrapolate the implications of the cultivation of plants and the domestication of animals, we can begin to see the further possibility of cultural revolution. Darwin focused on unconscious evolution and affirmed the mutability of species. I am focusing on conscious reformation and affirm the transformability of communities. Within societies, variation is achieved through conscious cultivation of plants and domestication of animals. Likewise, conscious transformation of cultures occurs and has had revolutionary consequences. Historically, social reconstruction of cultures has occurred time and again. Too often, and increasingly, all these types of transformation have been in the direction of homogenization.

Now, homogenization threatens biological and cultural diversity and, as a consequence, it also threatens the quest for just communities. So, what is to be done? For the sake of the resiliency of the ecosystem and human societies, are we to simply affirm biological and cultural diversity in all their manifestations? This question has been answered in a variety of ways. Ronald Engel simply asserts a connection between biological and cultural diversity (1993, p. 189). Others regard one as leading to the other. Denis Goulet contends that biological diversity is needed for cultural diversity (1993), while William Lacy argues that cultural diversity is needed for biological diversity (1994).

The issue is not so much to address whether biological and cultural diversity are equi-primordial, or whether, at least now, one is the pre-condition for the protection of the other. Instead, the issue concerns not merely that they are interconnected, but also that common forces mutually threaten them. Should this realization lead to an unrestricted affirmation of diversity? As Steven Rockefeller has observed, "Just as some deep ecologists embrace a biocentric egalitarianism, so some multiculturalists demand that all cultures receive recognition of equal value" (1994, p. 94). I doubt we want to go this far, though determining the limits of tolerance is not easy (Wolff, Moore, and Marcuse, 1969).

An example of a position that goes too far in affirming unrestricted diversity can be found in David Hall. He affirms unrestricted diversity on biological, cultural, and metaphysical levels. Placing a priority on the cosmological over the ontological question, he states:

> As traditionally interpreted, both the cosmological and ontological questions presuppose an *ordered ground*. But the truly radical question is, in fact, the cosmological one, since it may receive the Nietzschean answer: There are only interpretations, perspectives, the sum of which is Truth, the sum of which is Chaos. (1987, p. 9)

Western metaphysics has viewed the world as one, as a single Cosmos. By contrast, the job Hall gives to metaphysics is, "to demonstrate how the alternative conceptions of order can receive balanced recognition in the articulation of a speculative vision" (ibid., p. 14). He uses these points to support unrestricted diversity, stating:

> Chaos as the sum of all orders is a Vast Indifference when assessed from the perspective of a class of uniform existences, established orders, or

selective criteria. As such, it is passive to an indefinite number of aims, ends and aspirations, and it sustains an indefinite number of "sorts" of things, providing privileged status to no single set of uniformities. The diverse particulars comprising the Vast Indifference that is original Chaos each establishes its own perspective on all others. At one end of the spectrum of existences, these particulars constitute the chaos of imagination; at the other end, they comprise the sum of all world-orders. (Ibid., p. 20)

Indeed, Hall celebrates diversity; at one point he states:

There is conflict, contradiction—chaos. Within this morass, the only metaphysical truth is that the totality of interpretations constitutes that which is. Added up, gathered together, interpretative perspectives provide truth. *Everything*, in the summative sense, is true. (Ibid., p. 4)

However, even if, metaphysically, all diversity arises from "the Vast Indifference of Chaos," I cannot be content with an unrestricted affirmation of diversity.

Sometimes, we cannot afford to be indifferent to, and tolerant of, natural events and cultural practices. For example, we are seeking to contain the AIDS virus, and we should seek to restrain ethnic cleansings. However, my concern is not so much with such limit cases to a philosophy affirming unrestricted diversity, as with the way in which some partial gains by multiculturalists and environmentalists can create a false sense that protection of cultural and biological diversity is genuine and adequate. To express my discontent, I now turn to an application of the distinction between negative and positive peace to the quest for diversity.

In this regard, André Gorz makes a distinction in the ecological field that parallels the one between negative and positive peace. He notes:

when, after exhausting every means of coercion and deceit, capitalism begins to work its way out of the ecological impasse, it will assimilate ecological necessities as technical constraints, and adapt the conditions of exploitation to them. (1980, p. 3)

This practice is like negative peace. Such environmental accommodation is like the concession to multiculturalism in the workplace.

Gorz next addresses a concept similar to positive peace. He asks:

what are we really after: A capitalism adapted to ecological constraints; or a social, economic, and cultural revolution that abolishes the constraints of capitalism and, in so doing, establishes a new relationship between the individual and society and between people and nature? Reform or revolution? (Ibid., p. 19)

Gorz notes, "without changing the technology, the transformation of society will remain formal and illusory" (ibid., p. 20).

I am not worried that we will suddenly witness a movement toward an unacceptable quest for unrestricted biological and cultural diversity. Instead, I am worried that gains made by environmentalists and multiculturalists will not go far beyond obtaining the minimum accommodations that the social system must make to maintain itself. Just as ending fighting is not sufficient, ending cultural and biological degradation is not sufficient.

3. Critique of Domination and Militarism

I began with the thesis that communities of justice should welcome diversity. Historically, communities have too often excluded diversity of one form or another—generally, of many forms, given the long-standing connection of communities with systems of privilege and domination, as well as militarism.

Johan Galtung suggests we have developed the capacity to destroy not only population groups, but also the social fabric and ecological system within which they are located and upon which they depend. He uses the terms "genocide," "sociocide," and "ecocide" to refer to these capacities and uses "omnicide" to refer to their combination (1982, p. 11). For over two decades, I have had reservations about the term omnicide (Gay, 1985). John Somerville coined the term and used it in his claim that the use of nuclear weapons would not be nuclear war but instead, "nuclear omnicide" 1985). Besides my factual reservation about whether all sentient life would be destroyed, I also have a linguistic one. I believe advocates of peace and justice need to avoid using terms that foster alienation (Gay, 1987). Instead, they should seek an understood language of inclusion (Gay, 1998b).

Beyond not being a part of everyday discourse, the term omnicide has problems like Bertrand Russell's earlier claim that, in nuclear war, all of humanity would parish. Somerville and Russell argue from an extreme that is as untenable as that of Russell's adversary Sidney Hook when he argued human beings would have no freedom under Soviet communism (Gay, 1990). As philosophers, we are better served by arguing from more, rather than less, defensible factual claims. Even if large-scale use of nuclear weapons would destroy all life, we do not have to postpone protest until the destruction of war raises the scepter of killing all life (Gay, 1989). Finally, use of this term incites fear. Hope has more staying power than fear (Gay, 2006).

For me, however, Galtung's appropriation of the term omnicide is less important than the conceptual links he makes among goals of peace, multiculturalism, and environmentalism, and, I would add, the quest for just communities. These goals are jeopardized by practices within the triad Galtung designates as the "environment-development-military systems triangle." He goes on to suggest we need a concept of security that encompasses military, developmental, and environmental systems. He rejects any attempt to separate consideration of the environment with consideration of security. I too see the negative connection of militarism to the environment (Gay, 1996).

Conversely, positive peace for a nation (and even more for the planet) aids biological and cultural diversity and obviously contributes to the creation of just communities. Just as advocates of peace and justice need to support multi-culturalism and environmentalism, even so advocates of biological and cultural diversity can come to a similar critique of the military-industrial complex.

4. Cultural Diversity In and Among Communities

I give a variety of reasons why communities need to embrace diversity. Beyond the need to promote biological diversity, welcoming communities also need to embrace a wide-range of cultural diversity, including differences in ability/disability, age, culture, ethnicity, gender, language, race, religion, sexual orientation, and socio-economic status. Sexism, heterosexism, racism, ethnocentrism, nationalism, and classism take many forms. These pervasive and pernicious forms of violence are expressed on personal and institutional levels, both overtly and covertly (Russ, 1983; Outlaw, 1992, p. 459; Cady, 1991; Comstock, 1991). Under these conditions, gender, sexual orientation, ethnicity, and other components of personal and group identity can become social "marks" that hamper or even prevent the achievement of self-esteem, meaning, and other positive values (Gay, 2007b). At the extreme, these characteristics can be a "mark" for death.

However, the issue of community and diversity is not just internal to each particular community. While in principle, a diversity of just communities is possible, in practice, the issue of justice among a plurality of communities also needs to be addressed. Nevertheless, as Walter Bryce Gallie has noted, "No political philosopher has ever dreamed of looking for the criteria of a good state vis-à-vis other states" (1978, p. 140).

As I have stated elsewhere, in relation to the quest for global peace and justice, we need not only a welcoming of diversity within communities but also among global communities (2010). I recognize that the current geopolitical climate makes the achievement of such a welcoming of diversity among global communities rather difficult. Consider just the last decade of the twentieth century and the first decade of the twenty-first century. Shortly after the disintegration of the Soviet Union at the close of 1991, United States officials began to promote the mantra of "democracy and market economy" (Gay, 2004, p. 122). This mantra meant democracy in the political sphere and non-democratic capitalism in the economic sphere. Then, after 11 September 2001, the new mantra became "9/11 and the 'war on terrorism'" (Gay, 2007a, p. 29). This new mantra promotes the view that preventing another terrorist attack justifies many measures that otherwise would require serious examination.

Both mantras relate to containment. Between 1992 and 2001, the mantra of democracy and market economy meant that governments were to keep out challenges to democracy and to keep out challenges to capitalism. Since 2001, the mantra of "9/11 and the 'war on terrorism'" has meant keeping terrorists from attacking democratic governments and capitalist economic interests. Neither one of these mantras promotes the type of welcoming of diversity among global communities that I am advocating. In recent years, I have argued for economic democracy (2004; 2006), and for over a decade, I have argued for nonviolent approaches to national security (1994).

Earlier, I connected Darwin's work with the prospect for seeing how social transformation can be undertaken, even to the point of cultural revolution. With respect to the possibility of transformation on a global scale toward the welcoming of diversity among global communities, one issue that we need to address is whether modern societies are locked into the type of iron cage described by Max Weber in his 1900 *Economy and Society* (1968). Has the homogenization I described earlier ended transformation? Francis Fukuyama may think so (1992). I do not (1998b).

Elsewhere, I have argued (1976, p. 19) that, philosophically, an important question remains unanswered by Weber: after Weber delimited a theory of society which accounts for the transformations up to modern society, why did he stop with the historical acceptance of the present structure of societies and the relations among them? The same question can be posed to Fukuyama. Just as I am opposed to linguistic determinism (1999, pp. 28–29), I am opposed to the view that we cannot transform global communities into ones that welcome diversity (1998a). I hardly claim to know how to achieve such transformation, but I contend it is possible.

Immanuel Kant reminded us that peace is possible in his 1795 *Perpetual Peace*, and, for this reason, he argued that we have a moral duty to seek to advance it (1983). Of course, while making this important point, Kant accepted a form of world federalism that denies a means of intervention against nation states that practice unacceptable forms of diversity in which basic human rights are denied; I have argued that where such extremes should not be tolerated, nonviolent forms of intervention are possible (2000). Likewise, I contend here that just communities that welcome diversity are possible, and, I further contend we have a moral duty to seek to achieve them.

Even if some just communities are attained, this achievement will be only partial and precarious unless and until a plurality of just global communities are able to welcome their respective and distinctive ways of affirming diversity.

Two

FROM SCAFFOLD TO PRISON TO NURSERY:
THE SHAME OF PUNISHMENT

Wendy C. Hamblet

Punishment, following Thomas Aquinas, is defined as "the infliction of a penal evil by a legitimate authority upon one who has committed an [offense]" (*Summa Theologica* Art. 1, Obj. 5). Punishment is an evil. What distinguishes it from the evil done by private individuals, as you or me, is that it is committed by a "legitimate authority." However, ancient tragedy long ago challenged this facile identification, showing that authority is itself legitimated, not simply by the fact of holding power—any tyrant can do that—but by ruling rightly, a crucial aspect of which is "right punishing." Sophocles's *Antigone* (c. 442 BCE), and Aeschylus's *Oresteia* (c. 458 BCE) and especially *Prometheus Bound* (c. 480–410 BCE under dispute) explore the connection between political legitimacy and right punishment (see Benardette, Grene, and Lattimore, 196; Sophocles, 2003).

The true statesman demonstrates the right to rule by evidencing a kind of knowledge or expertise, what Plato calls the science of right measure. Rightful rulers measure rightly, including in the case of punishments—not too much, not too little, not the wrong kind, not to the wrong parties, not arbitrary forms of evil nor evil for arbitrary reasons, such as private gain or pleasure or revenge. The legitimate evils people call "punishment" are caught up in elaborate systems of political and social tradition, regulated to the minutest detail as to their attending circumstances. That is to say, punishment is a ritual, bound up with the identity of the group.

So it is of pivotal significance that Plato's statesmen, the expert in the science of measure, rejects the use of punishment altogether; the statesman does not punish. Instead the statesman follows Socrates's counsel to his accusers in *The Apology* (Plato, c. 399 BCE), taking aside the offender, as parent to child or doctor to patient, and educating the epistemologically challenged, guiding the misguided aright. For the ancient philosophers, a carefully regulated education including fitting exemplars is the only way to cultivate citizen virtue and keep people from going astray into criminality. If punishment must be applied, its function is curative alone.

When criminologists ask, "What Works?" with regard to punishment, they arrive at much the same answer as did the ancients (McGuire, 1999). Nothing works very well, but education is the single only response that seems to have the slightest effect on recidivism. In the United States, the vast majority of criminals incarcerated in prisons are sadly lacking in education, many of them unable to read and write. Yet since the 1990s, grants supporting criminal education have been abandoned. Many Western states, such as Canada, have highly curative prison systems, with much educational opportunity and the expected result of low recidivism rates, but others, such as the United States, herd their miscreants into overcrowded, under-funded prisons where, further dehumanized, they are granted a rigorous education—in criminality—trained in, rather than cured of, their soul-sickness, injustice.

If we trust Aquinas's definition of punishment, then any punishment exacted lawfully is just, even in the aforementioned case where punishment has undeniably ill effects. On the other hand, if we trust Plato and accept that justice is a virtue and that virtues are known by their good effects, we would be forced to admit that punishment is not in itself a good, not an ideal form; punishment enjoys no lofty distinction as an unqualified good, but *participates* in the form of justice, only to the extent that its virtue is manifest in favorable effects. Thus current penal methods do not warrant their distinction as a good. Though we may not be willing to go so far as to agree with Socrates in the *Gorgias*, when he insists that it is never just to do harm to anyone, we must at least agree on the softer Platonic point that justice can be said to occur only where punishment achieves the desired objective of curing the soul of the unjust person. Since current popular methods of punishment do not, and are not intended to, cure the sickened souls of prisoners, they cannot be said to exemplify justice. Indeed since they actually effect harm, rather than good, they must exemplify a lack of justice—injustice.

How did we arrive at the current state of affairs where, in the name of justice, we are employing punitive injustice, disregarding the overwhelmingly ill effects on individual deviants and on society in general, as recidivism rates spiral out of control and crime spills out of the jails and into the streets? I have said that punishment is a ritual by definition, because it comes to be regulated to its minutest detail according to strictly determined principles of observance. It is the very nature of ritual that it is carried out automatically, blindly. We do things this way because we have done things this way for a very long time and so alternative ways of doing things do not come into view *as possibility* in our everyday observances of things, until some unforeseen event arises on the horizon of the lifeworld and causes a paradigm shift that opens us to new possibilities.

Right now we can barely envision any better way of running a human community, whether a family, a classroom, a sub-community, or a state, than by laws and investigations and trials and minions of control and enforcement, and punishments of a specific kind—bloodless, disciplinary incarcerations (from "time-outs" for toddlers, to "groundings" for teens, to isolation or labor in prisons for social offenders). But how did we come to accept *just these practices* so fully that we import them into the nursery?

To answer the question, it is helpful to assume a philosophical orientation employed by philosophers such as Friedrich Nietzsche and Michel Foucault, who trace histories of social phenomena, in the form of an "archeology of knowledge." But since the archeologist is always already implicated in the fields of power and knowledge relations that must be untangled, then "genealogy" raises the methodological bar a notch above mere archaeology, not merely illuminating how subjects experience phenomena, but mapping out the power-knowledge networks that determine the way subjects experience things, how they perceive the institutions they are endorsing at the time when those institutions come into being. Foucault explains the new orientation:

> In order to conduct a concrete analysis of power relations, one would have to abandon the juridical notion of sovereignty [which] presupposes the individual as a subject of natural rights or original powers. . . . Instead of asking ideal subjects what part of themselves or what powers of theirs they have surrendered, allowing themselves to be subjugated (*se laisser assujettir*), [the genealogist] would need to inquire how relations of subjectivation can manufacture subjects. (Foucault, 1997, p. 51)

Foucault's history of the prison, offered in *Discipline and Punish* (1995), performs a genealogical study of evolving attitudes toward punishment, to understand the current broad acceptance of the prison as the most humane and enlightened punitive form. So he returns to the time and the place where subjects first embraced this institution. He sees the use of prisons rather suddenly emerging at the turn of the nineteenth century, to replace the horrifying public spectacles of torture and execution that had been the norm of punishment, according to his reckoning, only a few short decades before.

Foucault opens *Discipline and Punish* against the backdrop of these horrific punishments by straightway plummeting the reader into a phenomenological experience of the medieval torture spectacle. The strategic position assigned to the *Pièces originales* (describing the sentence administered to Damiens, the regicide) in Foucault's genealogical study is designed, not merely to coolly convince the reader about his penal theory, but to drag the culprit *affectively* through the sensibilities that punitive excesses evoke. The reader is forced to experience the shock, disgust, and shame that Foucault will claim bring cruel punishments to an end. Witness the affective labor that his opening descriptions work upon your sensibilities.

On 2 March 1757, Damiens, the regicide, was condemned:

> to make the *amende honorable* before the main door of the church of Paris," where he was to be "taken and conveyed in a cart, wearing nothing but a shirt, holding a torch of burning wax weighing two pounds. (Foucault 1995, p. 3)

and:

in said cart, to the Place de Grève, where, on the scaffold that will be
erected there, the flesh will be torn from his breasts, arms, thighs and
calves with red-hot pincers, his right hand, holding the knife with which
he committed the said parricide, burnt with sulphur, and, on those places
where the flesh will be torn away, poured molten lead, boiling oil, burning resin, wax and sulphur melted together and then his body drawn and
quartered by four horses and his limbs and body consumed by fire, reduced to ashes and his ashes thrown to the winds. (Ibid.)

Foucault drags us through the sentence, and then unfolds in gory detail
the chapters of its execution—the victim's pitiable cries to his god, the practical challenges of horse-drawn quartering that requires the intervention of
attendants to sever the limbs by hand, and finally the report that the poor culprit
was still alive when his limbless trunk was thrown on the stake for burning.
      We are shocked and repulsed by the tale. Then, with a segue of but three
little words ("eighty years later"), Foucault casts us into another time and
place, another world of "penal style"—bureaucratized, rationalized, con-
trolled, examined, and managed to the most minute detail. A page and a half
description details but a single day in the life of a prisoner. The reader experiences a flood of relief at the shift to the new penal style, the horror fading
into mere boredom at the hyper-regulated day of the prison inmate. Surely
this is the civilized alternative, the reader breathes. Foucault comments on the
new configurations of justice and punishment:

the great institutional transformations, the formulation of explicit, general codes and unified rules of procedure; with the almost universal
adoption of the jury system, the definition of the *essentially corrective*
character of the penalty and the tendency, which has become increasingly marked since the nineteenth century, to *adapt punishment to the individual offender*? (Ibid., pp. 7–8, emphasis added)

But how did we get from here to there, from the horrors of public execution to the tedious trivialities of a long prison day? Foucault attributes this
dramatic shift in the mechanisms of justice and penology to an attitude shift
in the public audience:

Now the scandal and the light are to be distributed differently; it is the
conviction itself that marks the offender with the unequivocally negative
sign; the publicity has shifted to the trial; the execution itself is like an
additional shame that justice is ashamed to impose on the condemned
man. (Ibid., p. 9)

Enlightenment ideals, argues Foucault, have in a few short decades reconfi-
gured the logic of shame in public sentiments in Western states. Public sensi-

bilities drive punishments from the scaffold into dungeons, labor camps, ships' bellies, and fields.

Like the good Leontius ascending from the Piraeus, the public has become ashamed of the desires for punitive carnage after which their eyes had thirsted. But instead of chastising their eyes, as Leontius did when they (his eyes) gloated at the rotting corpses thrown over the walls of Athens, the Western public of the early nineteenth century project the shame in their penal tastes onto the executioner, and from him to the legitimating authority that fed their savage tastes, by legislating cruel and bloody spectacles (Plato, *Republic*, 4.439e). Because shame indicates moral failure, the challenge to the edifice of power presented by the people's shame was a moral challenge. Moral arguments always question not only the rightfulness of an act, but the rightfulness of the actor. It challenges legitimacy.

In naming the public spectacle shameful, its audience was challenging the system of justice and the entire hierarchy of state power that stands behind the henchman. For Foucault, everyone has grown shame-full, with the exception of the criminal, who has become the object of public pity and the victim of a barbaric system. Suddenly—over "a few decades," according to Foucault (1995, p. 8)—detested criminal is transformed into pitiable victim of a brutal system. The moral debt to the convict is made good through the application of healing therapies ("essentially corrective") and an "army of experts" arises to concoct individualized remedies to set right the historical wrong.

Foucault's genealogy of punishment represents an ingenious study and his treatment of the shift in the economy of penal practice in modernity has located, in the element of shame, a key factor in the logic of punishment. We *felt* the evolution of shame that landed us in modern punitive practices, as we followed his horrifying chronology. However, while shame plays a central role in determining penology, in modern times as in ancient Western states, I will argue that its role is different from the one assigned to it by Foucault, and its ways are far more devious and debilitating. Foucault's explanation for the dramatic shift in penal practices, as the Western world enters the modern era, is overly generous, and grants to Westerners a sudden humaneness, a softening of their sensibilities, that they are unlikely to deserve.

Populations do not suddenly become ashamed of their taste for bloody mutilations and cruel executions; public shame follows the revolution, rather than precedes it. Certainly the French and American Revolutions shifted the terms of judicial discourse from "sin" and "indecency" to "rights" and "liberties," a shift in the conceptual universe that opened the door to new theories of justice. However, the shift in attitude that brought an end to executions, except in the most heinous of crimes, had a different source than Enlightenment ideals—another, far more practical explanation.

While no community is monolithic, public sentiment, even at the base of the social ladder, tends to reflect the interests of the ruling classes, because who, more than the dispossessed and marginalized, need so desperately to belong to the system? Public opinions about what is shameful and what is honorable tend to serve power, rather than to challenge it, in this historical era as in every other. Shame is a far more conservative force and works in far more complex ways than Foucault allows.

Foucault, the genealogist, explains the penal shift this sympathetic way, because he suffers from the influence of a pervasive Western power/knowledge force, the myth of "history as progress." He gets wrong the economy of punishment and the logic of shame, because he misdates the revolution and compacts its duration into a few short decades. The shift was much more gradual and organic than Foucault appreciates, and begins two hundred years earlier than he asserts. The mistaken dating and compressed duration of the revolution in penal tempers conceals from the genealogist's view the slow but steadily growing forest of revolutionary ideology for the sudden flash of late-born ideological trees (Enlightenment ideals).

Let us step further back in history, to the thirteenth century displacements and enclosures (began in the thirteenth century and peaked in the sixteenth) that evidence the breakdown of the stable social relationships that had held the feudal world intact. Marjorie Rowling describes those tight-knit webs of social relations in her classic study of *Life in Medieval Times*:

> Everyone owed services and obligations of some sort to those below and above them . . . . without the work done by serfs on the manorial estates the whole fabric of medieval agriculture, on which monasticism and feudalism were built, would have collapsed. (1979, p. 42)

The richly interwoven tapestry of human life, the paternalistic ethos of the baron, and church teachings on poverty and charity granted positive moral connotation to the condition of poverty in this era. Indeed if shame was to be found, it was attached, not to the condition of poverty, but to its neglect. The hardworking "noble ploughman" was eulogized in medieval art, poetry, and song, while the unfortunate beggar of the early Middle Ages offered opportunity for the wealthy and the religious to practice *caritas* (charity).

From the thirteenth through the sixteenth century, the stable relationships of feudal times gave way to the wage labor relations of capitalism and the individualistic ethic of the capitalist. Populations swelled and the poor, pushed off their plots and common lands, flooded into European cities; natural disasters of fire, disease, and failed crops rendered food supplies precarious and plagues grew commonplace in the overcrowded cities. As times got tougher, the indigent homeless, outlaws, witches, Jews, gypsies, and foreigners came under increasingly brutal persecution by lay populations, as much as by legalized authorities.

The lawmakers of Europe responded to the mounting problems posed by hordes of homeless indigents, by refocusing the law to criminalize the specific practices of the poor—vagrancy, prostitution, petty property crimes, and

banditry. Almost every crime became punishable by the death penalty, exacted in drawn-out public spectacles. Rows of swinging corpses of vagabonds
were strung up for miles along the roadsides of late medieval cities to deter
the miserable masses.

These spectacles served a number of practical purposes, from trimming
the population from the bottom, to providing convenient scapegoats for the
indignation of the wealthy, the ascetic disgust of the bourgeoisie, as well as
the general wretchedness of the lower classes, wallowing in an atmosphere of
oppression, desperation, and hopelessness, alongside obscene extremes of
wealth. The public spectacle of cruel and bloody punishments arose, not
simply as a legal or political trend, but as a public sport and a diversion from
the difficulties of the times.

These public brutalities not only failed to elicit public shame, but shame
functioned in a much more devious way to exacerbate the situation. Just as
the conditions of the poor slipped to depths of misery unparalleled in centu-
ries, the Protestant religions came into their own, importing into the public
consciousness a new worldview and a new shame-based ethic (Weber, 2002).
As Max Weber's brilliant study illuminates, the "Protestant Ethic" of the
bourgeois entrepreneurs, who filled the ranks of the rising middle classes in
European societies, propagated a rigorous ideology that identified their own
characteristics—intelligence, industriousness, and economic asceticism—as
the marks of god's faithful. In short, worldly success, accumulation of capital,
became the indicator of god's grace.

A logical consequence of the Protestant Ethic was the assignation of negative moral connotation to the condition of impoverishment. The poor came to
be seen as morally decadent, dishonest, foul, untrustworthy, lazy, and deserv-
ing of their lot. The poor, bad *by nature*, were a social disease that needed to
be contained in prisons or wiped out on the gallows. Almsgiving only exacer-
bated the problem, because the lazy poor would only work if they were forced
to do so by dire circumstances. The poor are not poor because god so ordered
the world that every creature has its proper place, intrinsic value, special
function and dignity within the whole; the poor fail because economically
grinding times sift the wheat from the chaff and expose the morally faulty.

The era of cruel public punishments that arose in the late Middle Ages
parallels the over-abundance of human life and the penury of opportunities
for gainful employment. As the number of available working bodies increased, wages plummeted, jobs grew scarce, and people turned to crime, as
people always do in hard economic times. Justice, punishment, and public
sentiments responded with predictable cruelty to the plentiful poor.

However, by the end of the sixteenth century, the times had turned
again. The populations of Europe dwindled, creating a severe shortage of
unskilled, manual laborers, and wages began to rise. Normally, this situation
would be expected to increase the value placed on human life and to improve
both wages and public attitudes toward the poor. But global capitalism was

just at this moment in its budding stage, and the burgeoning entrepreneurial class rising across Europe could not plow forward with their new globalizing enterprises, if wages continued to soar. Since the entrepreneurial worldview configured the "lazy" poor as undeserving of, and morally ill-served by, higher wages and better working conditions, the challenge became how to secure their labor, against their indolent wills, without paying them the higher wages which would tempt them to work fewer hours, while also eroding the investment capital fueling budding global adventures.

The legislators and the machinery of justice leapt to the challenge and rounded up the vagrant and the beggar. The gallows were exchanged for the prison, and the prison was transformed into a manufactory, or the prisoner was chained out of sight in the ship's galley and transported to the colonies to build a New World. The philosophical discourses of the times figured the criminal as the monster who fit better with the savages overseas than infecting civilized society.

The new mechanisms of justice and punishment followed the example of the "houses of correction" that arose as early as 1555 in London and swept across every country of Europe by 1576 to take the lazy poor in hand (ibid., p. 41). Houses of correction absorbed vagrants, beggars, prostitutes, idlers, and thieves, but also took in "ne'er-do-well children and spendthrift dependents" for a handsome fee (ibid., p. 43). Neither the houses of correction nor the new laws and punishments arose because people were ashamed of how they treated the poor; they were designed expressly, as Georg Rusche and Otto Kirchheimer put it, in their classic study, as places "where those who were unwilling were forced to make their everyday practice conform to the needs of industry" (ibid.), p. 42.

Over the subsequent century, military recruiters got on board, pointed the way. "Press gangs" made their appearance, about the time of the Thirty Years War (1618–1648); army officers of Frederick II's Prussia began seizing passers-by and "pressing" them into military service. Later, "orphans, bastards, beggars, and paupers" in infirmaries were forcefully recruited (Rusche and Kirchheimer, 1939, p. 216n22). Ultimately, the army turned to criminal labor to pad their ranks. Before long across Europe, armies became indistinguishable from penal organizations, enlisting not only from their own prisons, but from the prisons of foreign countries as well. It was only a matter of time before the shrewd entrepreneurial minds of the sixteenth century thought to exploit this avenue of cheap labor for them.

My earlier dating for the penal revolution is supported not only by the chronology of historical events just noted, but also accords with the timing of the growing hegemony of Protestant ideas. Martin Luther's "Ninety-Five Theses on Power and the Efficacy of Indulgences" (1957), exposing abuses of Roman Catholic clergy, including the sale of "indulgences" (extracting large sums of money from wealthy parishioners as a means of buying freedom from God's punishments for sins), launched the Protestant Reformation in Europe (1517). John Calvin was preaching that "God helps them what helps themselves" just as the houses of correction came into being. It is hardly surprising that the development of correction houses reached its peak in Holland, which, at the end of the sixteenth century, was both a Protestant stronghold and "the most highly developed capitalist system in Europe" (Rusche and Kirchheimer, 1939, p. 216n22).

Foucault claims that a new and general sense of shame is responsible for replacing public and brutal punishments with more humane "disciplinary" methodologies. But this claim is overly generous to the populations of early modern Europe. The penal shift relentlessly followed the logic of the stark utilitarian ideology of the entrepreneurs, industrialists, and monarchs who held sway in the early capitalist period. Public shame did not protect the criminalized impoverished; on the contrary, shame criminalized poverty to extract its unpaid labor.

Prisons persist in the twenty-first century, not only because poverty and unemployment persist and human life is cheap. They persist because shame is not revolutionary, but doggedly conservative. We cannot shift back our penal tastes once the revolution has occurred, so we are unable to return to killing off the poor, despite global overpopulation and dwindling jobs; so rows of swinging corpses along Park Avenue and les Champs-Élysées is out. The Protestant Ethic remains intact because it remains highly functional in our times, though it has grown subtle, secularized, and sublimated in the public consciousness. Shame is still attached to the condition of poverty, both by the wealthy and by the poor themselves. This is because shaming the poor for their condition is highly functional: it places the burden of social change upon the lower classes.

The longstanding prejudice that distinguishes the poor as shameful and the economically successful as morally worthy is simply a ruse, invented by the powerful to justify the gross inequities of their societies, and to keep wages minimal and profits high, while concealing the greed which drives the system. There is an abundance of evidence to show that when people are given the resources they need for success, they will rarely disappoint their dreams. But when people grow hopeless for success by legitimate avenues, they will indeed turn to alternative survival strategies—cheating, stealing, and selling drugs and their flesh.

Criminality is tied up with social injustice; criminal law targets the petty crimes that bleed out the bottom of the social ladder, onto the streets, and into the prisons, and then tumbles back out into the streets. What comes to define criminality is determined by prevailing prejudices, so the real crime, the global networks that feed war, enslave women and children, topple governments, and support corporate hegemony are eclipsed by tired moralizations about the decadence of the poor, the bicycle thief, and the drug addict. Rusche and Kirchheimer conclude their brilliant study of penology in the West with the following scathing indictment of modern societies:

So long as the social consciousness is not in a position to comprehend and act upon the necessary connection between a progressive penal system and progress in general, any project for penal reform can have but doubtful success, and failures will be attributed to the inherent wickedness of human nature rather than to the social system. The inevitable consequence is the return to the pessimistic doctrine that man's evil nature can be tamed only by depressing the prison standard below that of the lowest classes. The futility of severe punishments and cruel treatment may be proved a thousand times, but so long as society is unable to solve its social problems, repression, the easy way out, will always be accepted. It provides the illusion of security by covering the symptoms of social disease with a system of legal and moral value judgments. (1939, p. 207)

Discourses of human nature underpin ideologies of social control (however subtle), and justify social inequalities. Without a natural reason for the differences that separate the lot of the impoverished from the lot of the wealthy, we would have to fall back on explanations of sheer luck and historical injustice to explain why some people live lives that are brutish and short, while others drive Mercedes to their summer homes in the Hamptons.

So are certain styles of punishment the problem, or is punishment *per se* a mistaken response to the problem of social deviance in the lower classes? Studies show that when the conditions of the poor improve, as societies become more prosperous, lower class crime tends to fall away. The United States is the conspicuous exception to this rule, because it has the most unequal distribution of wealth among all industrialized societies. But studies expose the tendency for punishment to backfire and defeat the purposes for which it is instituted. Foucault, the genealogist, should have better appreciated that precisely because power and knowledge are not merely coercive but relational, coercive responses to crime *inspire* resistances, stimulate crime, and dehumanize punished and punisher.

An extensive study of the effects of punishment, conducted by Benedikt Herrmann, Christian Thöni, and Simon Gätcher (University of Nottingham School of Economics) across sixteen ethnically and economically diverse participant pools around the globe, showed that people from a variety of backgrounds behave much the same way when they are being subjected to punishment (2008, pp. 1362–1367). In their experiments, the participants played a "public goods game" with and without a "punishment component." The public goods game is a stylized model of situations that require cooperation to achieve socially beneficial outcomes; examples include paying taxes, voting, cooperative hunting, neighborhood watches, recycling programs, climate change, and many other forms of teamwork. The common feature is that cooperation leads to a shared beneficial outcome but is endangered by selfish incentive to free-ride on others' contributions.

The findings of the experiment are compelling. While "punishing beha-viors" varied broadly across the groups, some findings were consistent. The experiment bore out the common assumption that punishing negative beha-viors does have some observable effects in motivating the socially under-cooperative to alter their ways. But the behavior change inspired was not the simple rehabilitation that is generally expected. The experiment consistently demonstrated that, in those groups, which were permitted to punish, punish-ing tended to elicit a "highly significant increase in antisocial punishment across all participant pools as a function of the amount of punishment re-ceived in the previous period" (ibid., pp. 1363–1364). That is to say, when groups used punishment to motivate members in the direction of cooperative behavior, the result was precisely the opposite of the desired objective: un-cooperative behavior proliferated and the undeserving, those who were al-ready cooperating, came to be targeted for punishment.

The test broadly confirmed:

the presence of a punishment opportunity had dramatic consequences on the achieved cooperation levels. . . . Differences in cooperation across participant pools are significantly negatively related to antisocial pu-nishment: the higher the antisocial punishment is in the participant pool, the lower is the average cooperation level in that participant pool. (Ibid.)

In sum, when societies resort to the gentlest punishments to force coop-erative behaviors, punishing tends to proliferate from the just to the antiso-cial, and to drive the entire society to withdraw from cooperative behaviors. The scientists conclude, contrary to previous experiments in the United States and Europe: "the cooperation-enhancing effect of a punishment opportunity cannot be taken for granted (ibid.)."

This experiment helps us to show us that punishment is useless for the purpose of stimulating cooperative behaviors. It shows that punishments in-stead have an ill effect not only on the criminals but on the societies outside the prisons. It indicates as well that punitive violence is consistent with other violence; it has a strong propensity to rebound, both inside and outside prison walls, infecting everyone in the society. By this account, both crime and pu-nishment may be considered social diseases that proliferate and contaminate whole societies. However, this valuable experiment does not tell us *why* pu-nishment has these negative effects across the societies in which it is prac-ticed (except to speculate that punishments may stimulate the desire for re-venge). I argue that the dangerous factor in punishment that causes it to be-tray the goals it seeks to achieve is the very factor Foucault credits with civi-lizing penal practices—shame.

The use of shame for ethical conditioning has a long and time-honored history. The Greek tradition hails shame as a useful moral teacher; Agamem-non confirms the socio-military hierarchy when he shames Achilles by taking

his beautiful war bride. Socrates is ashamed to sneak out of the prison, even
to save his life. Shame underpins the humility ethos of the philosopher, as
well as the honor code of the warrior. It underseats as well the Talmudic tradition of aporetic hermeneutics in Jewish ethics. From the Greeks and the
Jews, the tradition finds its way into Christianity, in the asceticism of priests
against which Nietzsche's Zarathustra rails, and in the shame that gathers
around sex and the bodily functions.

Postmodern philosophers, such as Emmanuel Lévinas and Jacques Derrida, seek to depart from the Greek tradition, but they too ground their ethics
in aspects of shame—guilt, apology, mourning (Hamblet, 2010). Shame is a
useful pedagogical tool for instilling prohibitions. Anthropologists of violence assure us that the lessons learned in pain are the lessons most deeply
learned, and shame is a form of emotional pain that teaches people deeply.
But let's be certain this pedagogical tool is the best that ethics can do before
importing it to the nursery to teach moral behavior.

Shame is a sting felt in the depth of the soul that alerts one to one's
moral failure. We feel ashamed for a moral fault that offends our sense of
what we *ought* to be doing, the code of moral duty or behavior endorsed by
our local community. Because we know what we ought or ought not be
doing, we enjoy the benefit of shame's moral alert. Shame sounds the warning bell, stops us in our tracks, interrupts and paralyzes our spontaneous freedom. If we continue on our deliberative course despite shame's warning, or if
it arrives too late because we cannot foresee and control the infinite effects of
our acts, then shame can seep down to the innermost depths of our being, and
radically undermine our sense of worth as a human being.

But shame is morally problematic. The paradox of shame is that it is an
emotional response which recognizes an ethical failure, which recognition is
only possible where there has preceded an epistemological success. We can
only feel guilty for moral failure, where we have achieved adequate moral
learning. We can measure how far we have morally fallen, because we have
knowledge of the conventional boundaries. Since shame can only occur
where moral lessons have already been learned, the morally ignorant are incapable of shame. This explains why Socrates warns Polus in the *Gorgias*,
"Hush, Polus!" when the latter declares a shameful opinion: that anyone
should be jealous of a man who is "killing or imprisoning or depriving [oth-
ers] of property" (*Gorg.* 468e). Polus is shaming himself with this blatant
celebration of injustice, yet he does not *know* enough to feel ashamed. He is
epistemologically challenged. He has not completed his moral lessons to the
point where shame can function to stop him short of his shameless words.

Polus is shaming himself, but he does not *know* that he is. He is also
shaming his teacher Gorgias, who is standing by, watching him speak imprudently. Socrates does not punish Polus. Rather, he does as he advises his accusers in the *Apology*; he counsels Polus as his child—"Hush, Polus!"—
trying to teach him the moral lesson he has missed (*Apol.* 26a). The shame

that attaches to Polus's act (of speaking imprudently) fails to do any moral labor here; it fails to stop short Polus's tongue. The moral paradox of shame is that it only teaches those who have already learned their moral lessons. It has no pedagogical power to alter the behavior of those who most need its lessons.

Shame has a further moral flaw, in that it is ontologically paradoxical. It is an empirical event (an affective confirmation of a transgressive act) that has *ontological* consequences. *What I have done* has implications for *who I am*, both in my self-estimation and in the estimation of my social group, where the moral rules originate. Under the disfiguring weight of shame, we become like the monster sea-god Glaucus, "whose first nature," Socrates tells us, "can hardly be made out by those who catch a glimpse of him, because the original members of his body are broken off and mutilated and crushed, and in every way marred by the waves" so that "he is more like some wild creature than what he was by nature" (*Rep.* X.611d). Shame raises the question: *what kind of creature am I* that I have done this thing? Shame dehumanizes; it causes an ontological fall.

Shame is a moral teacher who teaches only those who do not need its lessons. But shame has greater flaws than its ineffectiveness on tyrants and fools. The greatest danger is that those members of the moral choir to whom shame is actively preaching can easily over-learn their lessons. Shame's ontological demotion gnaws away at the morally learned heart, destroying the morally sensitive soul, and disfiguring the moral fiber. Good people can take shame's warning too deeply to heart, and can retire, as Achilles, from the moral battlefield, or throw themselves on the side of the enemy, as the shamed Alkibiades did, when he found his inappropriate love for Socrates to be shameworthy.

Shame is a useful moral tool if it warns us, as Socrates's *daimonion* does, in advance of a moral lapse. It can boost our moral confidence, help us to be more effective exemplars to the morally struggling. But where the error is made and cannot be undone, shame is unhelpful in going forward. It is just one of the many debilitating affects—resentment, hatred, blame, envy, greed—that undermine people's fundamental joy in existence, their sense of worth, and their capacity to relate to others compassionately.

Yet this is precisely the moral tool we wield against those we wish to bring into the fold of cooperative society. Punishments were moved from the scaffold to the prison to the nursery, because for altering behavior, shame is a far more effective tool than scarring and maiming bodies; shame instills a *soul deep* alteration in offenders. But the changes it instills are counterproductive to the goals we seek to accomplish in punishing, leaving its victims ontologically and morally broken, in some cases beyond repair. The prisons, as the nurseries, must find more humane, more nurturing methods of guiding their foundlings to moral and psychological health.

Three

REPRESSIVE JUSTICE: MARCUSE, ADORNO, AND THE AMERICAN ATTEMPT TO LIVE WRONG LIFE RIGHTLY

Arnold L. Farr

1. Introduction: Justice and Its Discontents

Justice is very difficult to talk about in our society. For that matter, any moral or ethical concepts that have liberation as their purpose are difficult to talk about. With respect to justice, quite often confusion arises between a moral or ethical conception of justice and a juridical or legal one. The confusion lies in conflating what is the case (in terms of legal statutes) and what ought to be the case (in terms of ethical ideals).

Immanuel Kant's insight in the *Metaphysics of Morals* (2000, p. 3) was correct. The division between the Doctrine of Right and the Doctrine of Virtue is based on the problem of unifying moral law with human freedom and desire. Simply put, if all human beings chose to follow the moral law as presented by the categorical imperative, the central philosophical concept of the *Metaphisics of Morals*, then a harmony of wills would result. This harmony of wills would establish something like a Kingdom of God on earth. The result would be a state of perpetual peace. No human being would use another merely as a means to an end. Every human being would respect the human dignity of others and would govern his or her actions and desires accordingly. We would be able to co-ordinate our actions and desires as equal members of an ethical community.

Kant was aware that many human beings would resist following moral law. Therefore, a legal system must be erected on the foundation of morality to protect the freedom of those who have freely chosen to follow the moral law from those who have chosen to not follow it. Hence, the legal system and its conception of justice would have as its goal the materialization of moral principles even if members of society have not adopted those principles.

Nothing is wrong with these Kantian principles themselves. The problem is with the construction of moral principles and the further development of a legal system based on those principles without an adequate consideration of the human condition. A purely formalistic moral theory is bankrupt in a lifeworld already constituted by oppressive social and political forces.

The founders of the United States, as well as most of our political leaders and academics, are in the same boat in which Kant sails: the boat of wrong life. I will explore this notion of wrong life in more detail later. Just let me say here that, in Kant's philosophy and in the minds of the founders, most of us do not qualify as fully human.

Karl Marx reminded us in "The German Ideology," "The ideas of the ruling class are in every epoch the ruling ideas" (2000, p. 192), meaning, the class that is the ruling material force of society is, at the same time, its ruling intellectual force. In this, we can easily replace class with race, gender, or sexual orientation. Simply put, the dominant social group has the power and necessary social mechanisms to determine the values, ideas, and laws that shape a society and its institutions. We have seen that at one point, the dominant social group even had the power to determine who was human.

Although we have witnessed many struggles for liberation as well as some victories, the sins of the founders are still with us and are deeply embedded in our institutions, legal and other sorts. Today, victims are still being produced by the long-term consequences of previous systems of injustice, exploitation, alienation, and dehumanization. We have not yet made a clear exit from the wrong life into which many social groups were forced during earlier stages of history.

Our failure to understand how history works in the construction of oppressive social conditions and identities is one of the ways wrong life is perpetuated. In this regard, I will briefly examine some key ideas in the works of Hans-Georg Gadamer and Pierre Bourdieu. Although the theoretical projects of Gadamer and Bourdieu are quite different and originate from different concerns, they both have developed some insights that are helpful for anyone engaged in critical discourse about power relations. Gadamer was not concerned with power relations, but his understanding of prejudice and tradition can help us understand the social and political sedimentation of negative forms of prejudice and power relations.

Gadamer's concept of effective history is a useful theoretical tool for understanding the long-term effects of past systems of oppression. We are historical beings. This is not to say that we are completely determined by historical circumstances. It means that we are greatly influenced by our historical situation. Even in the domain of science, our social, cultural, geographical, and political environment influences what appears to be worthy of inquiry. The world is interpreted from our place within it. Even our understanding of other people is often reduced to our own way of experiencing the world.

In *Truth and Method* (1988), Gadamer develops the idea of effective history within the context of challenging the view, developed and advocated by Enlightenment thinkers, that we could somehow acquire knowledge without prejudice. His point is that all knowledge claims are, to some degree, rooted in prejudice. By "prejudice," he simply means to pre-judge. That is, all inquiry takes place against a historical backdrop whereby investigators are guided by values, norms, and ideas that they have inherited from a particular tradition. Since Gadamer is more concerned with epistemological issues, his

book is not written as a work in social or political philosophy. Therefore, Gadamer is not focusing on social justice issues. Nonetheless, he does provide
us with important tools for developing a theory of justice.

The critique, and apparent defense, of prejudice is not a justification for
bigotry. Gadamer's point is that our epistemic positions are not simply value-
neutral. This is an important tool for understanding and eliminating bigotry.
One of the problems with the Enlightenment is that the celebration of value
neutrality, open mindedness, and freedom were all constructed within the
context of oppression.

Think about the social status of women, blacks, Native Americans, the
poor, and gays and lesbians during the development of the language of freedom, equality, and justice. Most of our highest social, political, and moral
values were constructed at a time when most of the human population was not
considered human. Hence, we have a historical process of value formation
within institutions that systematically excluded some social groups. The values produced were designed to protect the dominant social group. The Enlightenment promised freedom but restricted the domain of freedom to an
"elite" segment of humanity. The rest became the victims of history.

Although we have attempted in some ways to remedy the damage done
by past systems of oppression and the exclusion of certain social groups from
democratic decision making processes, we are nowhere near finished. The
change in law has led members of the dominant social group to believe that
we are all on an equal playing field. Many people think that we are finished
because of a few changes in the law. However, changes in the law do not really remedy the social conditions that perpetuate suffering stemming from
past forms of oppression. As Gadamer stated: "In our understanding, which
we imagine is so straight forward, we find that, by following the criterion of
intelligibility, the other presents himself so much in terms of our own selves
that there is no longer a question of self and other" (1988, p. 268).

In terms of social justice, those in power are often the people who benefit from the present order of things. These are the people who want to insist
that we are all equal now, that the playing field is level. They tend to believe
that people are poor or suffer because they make bad decisions, not because
they are still excluded from decision-making processes or that some social
mechanisms still disempower them.

How is oppression passed on even if the changed laws are more inclusive? It is to Pierre Bourdieu that we must turn for an answer. One of the
most important and useful theoretical constructs in Bourdieu's work is his
concept of the *habitus*, which in some ways bears a kinship with Gadamer's
notion of effective history. The *habitus* functions as a sort of historical, social, and political backdrop, from which meaning emerges. Much like effective history, it supplies us with tools for interpreting social reality and defines
our place and the place of others within that reality. For example, so-
cial/economic class is often taken to be based on a natural division between

groups of people. Both concepts—effective history and *habitus*—disclose the social mechanisms at work that produce and maintain class divisions.

The *habitus* is not only a structuring structure, which organizes practices and the perception of practices, but also a structured structure: the principle of division into logical classes, which organizes the perception that the social world is, itself, the product of internalization of the division into social classes. Each class condition is defined, simultaneously, by its intrinsic properties and by the relational properties it derives from its position in the system of class conditions. The system of class conditions is also a system of differences. Through this system of differences people are situated differently in terms of their ability to acquire certain social goods such as education, material goods, and social esteem (Bourdieu, 1996, pp. 170, 172).

Two ideas in this passage will be explored here, first, the notion of "the system of class conditions," and second, the "perception of practices." The system of class conditions explains the mechanisms by which social inequality is perpetuated even if it appears that everyone is equal by law. Bourdieu argues that we inherit four forms of capital—economic, social, cultural, and symbolic—that affect our life chances or life trajectory. Hence, inequality begins at birth and conditions the trajectory of individuals' lives.

Economic capital refers to a family's financial wealth and what it can pass on to future generations. Social capital refers to social status and social connections, which provide opportunities for social advancement. Cultural capital includes education, socially-constructed aesthetic sensibilities, and values. Symbolic capital is the perception that results from a combination of the first three forms of capital. For example, most of us are familiar with stories of young black men getting a heavier punishment for carrying the same amount of marijuana than their wealthy white counter-parts. Low economic status and black skin tend to symbolize a criminal disposition, while white skin and wealth symbolize goodness. The white kid caught with drugs has simply made a mistake. The black kid caught with the same amount of drugs is a criminal and must be taken off the street before our society is corrupted.

According to Bourdieu, all four forms of capital work in tandem to produce a system of class conditions that then affects the trajectory of an individual's life. The trajectory or possibility for individuals is shaped not only by the quantity of capital in its four forms that persons have as resources for self-development and self-determination, but also by the way individuals, as members of a particular social group, are perceived by their group and others. My argument here is that our conception of justice does not escape the structuring function of the *habitus*.

2. Repressive Justice

Today, we can go further than Marx's statement, "the ideas of the ruling class are in every epoch the ruling ideas." As I have elucidated elsewhere, now the ruling class reshapes even the ideas of the oppressed so that they lose their emancipatory function (Farr, 2008).

I will now briefly examine Herbert Marcuse's critique of repressive tolerance as an example of the problem at hand. Marcuse argues that, at the beginning of the modern period, the concept of tolerance emerged from struggles for liberation. This occurred most frequently within the context of religious domination. However, the concept of tolerance would continue to be used by a wide range of social groups seeking deliverance from their marginalized position in society. The problem is that the concept of tolerance was eventually taken up by members of dominant social groups and used as a tool to encourage the acceptance of their oppressive views and values. Discriminating tolerance was replaced by pure tolerance, tolerance for the sake of tolerance. This form of tolerance refuses to recognize power relations between individuals and social groups. It assumes a level playing field where all views are equal and where one view has no greater social consequences than another.

Unfortunately, a few years ago, the trustees of St. Joseph's University (where I worked at the time) invited Rick Santorum to be our Commencement speaker even though he had made some very negative remarks about homosexuals. Some members of the faculty (myself included) protested by walking out as Santorum stood to speak. Other faculty members criticized those of us who walked out for our intolerance. What my colleagues failed to recognize was that our protest was a response to intolerance, and not just to a difference of opinion. As a policy maker, Santorum was in a position to do harm to those whose sexual identity he did not like.

Further, if Santorum was invited as a speaker who could be questioned after his talk, we would have happily stayed. The occasion was a lecture and the conferring of an Honorary Doctorate degree without the consent of the faculty. Most of us would have been happy to engage Santorum in a democratic forum. Ironically, in his speech, Santorum portrayed himself as a victim for standing up for his beliefs. What about the beliefs of homosexuals? Santorum would go on to use the language commonly used by oppressed people when they are seeking tolerance. He also told the students to be true to themselves—advice that perhaps he meant only to apply to heterosexuals.

Lately in the academy, we have witnessed this kind of misuse of tolerance, as well as misuse of the first amendment, by David Horowitz and others with their push for an Academic Bill of Rights. First, the claim that the left is somehow taking over our colleges and universities is simply false and not worth debating. Second, the cry for toleration of so-called conservative views is antithetical to the objective of tolerance. It is not the case that conservatives merely represent one set of views among others and that does no more harm than others. In a society where inequality and injustice still loom large, it is anti-democratic and close-minded to suggest that all views—even those promoted by the most powerful in society—are equal. Equality of views and opinions in the context of wrong life is not possible.

My point here is that the concept of justice requires the same type of critique that Marcuse provides of tolerance. In a society where the ideas of the ruling class become the ruling ideas, quite possibly, what we call justice is, at its core, injustice. This is especially true in that justice is often reduced to the legal conception of justice, which is, itself, based on negative rather than positive rights. By negative rights, I simply mean the right to be left alone, to not be interfered with, and to have property protected. By positive rights, I mean the right to have property, the right to have access to the necessary resources for self-development and self-determination.

Here, I follow Iris Marion Young's two ideals of justice. In *Inclusion and Democracy* (2002), she defines self-development and self-determination as follows:

> I interpret the value of self-development along lines similar to the values Amartya Sen calls equality as capabilities. Just social institutions provide conditions for all persons to learn and use satisfying and expansive skills in socially recognized settings, and enable them to play and communicate with others or express their feelings and perspectives on social life in contexts where others can listen. Self-development in this sense certainly entails meeting people's needs for food, shelter, health care, and so on.

> Self-determination, the second aspect of justice as I understand it, consists in being able to participate in determining one's action and the condition of one's action; its contrary is domination. Persons live within structures of domination if other persons or groups can determine without reciprocation the conditions of their action, either directly or by virtue of the structural consequences of their actions. (Ibid., pp. 31–32)

Our popular conception of justice is based on the negative theory of rights as it is set up to protect those who have. It does not concern itself with those who do not have. Further, our society is structured in such a way that those who have continued to have and get more at the expense of the have-nots, and this is perfectly legal. I remind the reader here of my discussion of Kant at the beginning of this paper. Even Kant's view that the law is based on the principle of morality is naïve. This may be the way that it should be, but the evidence suggests otherwise. Moreover, even our moral concepts are tainted by our social situation.

Western society is Kantian insofar as it claims to support moral principles that are universal in nature. However, it is this assumption of universality that produces immorality or wrong life. The view that we are all morally bound by the same principles is correct at one level, but at another it problematically presupposes a kind of sameness that does not exist. Perhaps, all of us adopting and living by the same moral principles would be nice. This would not, however, produce a just society if justice means something like fairness and equal opportunity, and if it is connected to assuring all citizens that they have equal opportunity to the necessary resources for self-development and self-determination. A morality that focuses on universal principles, as Kant's does, and ignores real social differences and inequalities, perpetuates wrong life.

3. Wrong Life and the Façade of Justice

Something is fundamentally correct in the universal moral principles developed by Kant, but the social context of application is problematic. The very structure of our society appears to invalidate Kantian universal moral principles. I believe that J. M. Bernstein is correct, in the introduction to his book on Theodor W. Adorno, to situate Adorno's negative dialectics within the context of a Nietzschean type of nihilism. However, in the philosophies of Friedrich Nietzsche and Adorno, this nihilism cannot be reduced to a personal feeling or belief that each philosopher holds regarding life. The nihilism here is the result of a critical insight; it is reflected in a particular form of life. One is reminded of Nietzsche's claim that our highest values de-value themselves. Western society has itself become nihilistic. One is also reminded of Adorno and Max Horkheimer's critique of the enlightenment in *Dialectic of Enlightenment* (1993). The enlightenment goal of disenchantment produces further enchantment. The escape from myth leads to myth. Our highest values de-value themselves. Bernstein writes:

> Adorno believes that scientific and bureaucratic rationalism are, in their claim to totality, irrational in themselves, and hence that the meaning deficit caused by the disenchantment of the world is equally a rationality deficit. Only an expanded conception of reason which derives from a reinscription of conceptuality can lead to a reinscription of ethical meaning. But for Adorno to expand reason is to expand the scope and character of cognitive life, of knowing. It is toward a more capacious sense of cognition and thus reason that Adorno struggles with the concept lead us. (2001, p. 4)

In *Negative Dialectics* (1987), Adorno's critique of Western philosophy and the enlightenment is designed to expose the misuse of the concept or the process of conceptualization. The concept fails to do justice to lived human experience and therefore, restricts rather than expands knowledge. The philosopher first constructs concepts and then attempts to force human lived experience into the concepts. This very process leads to what some feminist and Africana philosophers would call epistemologies of ignorance. Mastery of the concept does not suggest an adequate understanding of the human condition.

It suggests a thorough misunderstanding of the human condition. I will say more about this form of abstraction in philosophy and connect it to theories of justice in the next section of this paper. Here, the point that I want to make, following Adorno, is, that for justice to be properly conceptualized and applied, an expansion of knowledge is required.

Adorno's point is that the concept does not adequately represent lived human experience because the concept is formed without proper examination of lived human experience. Adorno's *Negative Dialectics* reminds us of the battle cry of Edmund Husserl's phenomenology to focus on "the things themselves," by which he means the phenomena, or our conscious ideas of things, and not natural objects.

However, what it means to get to the things themselves and what the things are differs radically for the two thinkers. For Adorno, the thing is always radically other. It cannot be reduced to conceptual knowledge without remainder. Knowledge of the other's experience requires an examination of the historical and social constellation of which the other is a part. What has to be bracketed is our prior conceptual misunderstanding of the other. What are the implications of this type of thinking for a theory of justice?

It is apropos here to briefly discuss Walter Benjamin's, "Thesis on the Philosophy of History." The Ninth Thesis especially can be used to explicate Adorno's negative dialectics. Benjamin writes:

> A [Paul] Klee painting named "Angelus Novus" shows an angel looking as though he is about to move away from something he is fixedly contemplating. His eyes are staring, his mouth is open, his wings are spread. This is how one pictures the angel of history. His face is turned toward the past. Where we perceive a chain of events, he sees one single catastrophe which keeps piling wreckage upon wreckage and hurls it in front of his feet. The angel would like to stay, awaken the dead, and make whole what has been smashed. But a storm is blowing from Paradise; it has got caught in his wings with such violence that the angel can no longer close them. This storm irresistibly propels him into the future to which his back is turned, while the pile of debris before him grows skyward. This storm is what we call progress. (1969, pp. 257–258).

Read from the perspective of negative dialectics, history, which is told by the victors of history, not the victims, is interpreted along the lines of an identitarian logic, which sees history as a unified and progressive chain of events. Even the notion of progress is formed in the minds of the victors and then improperly applied to history. The interpretation of history by the victors of history makes visible only what the victors want to make visible. They conceal, repress, and make voiceless that which really discloses what is going on. Identity has its beginning in non-identity. Progress is the piling up of ruins, broken and destroyed bodies/lives, distorted identities, and mutilated subjectivity.

The angel of history sees history as it is because the angel has been stripped of the traditional concepts provided by the victors of history. The angel sees the non-identity upon which identity constructs itself. History then is no longer seen as a mere chain of events, but as the perpetuation of wrong life. In this context Bernstein, following Adorno's critique of modernity, writes:

> The project of modernity has failed politically and ethically. Politically it has failed at least to provide all the inhabitants of the democratic states of Europe and North America with liberty, equality, and the freedom from fear and hunger it promised in its founding (Bernstein, p.40).

He continues:

> Modern, secular reason is self-undermining. Its self-undermining character has impacted on our practical life not only because it makes suspect the ethical ideals we employ to orient ourselves through the world, but because they are suspect lose their *force*, their power to (rationally) motivate and guide. The condition of nihilism is the interpretation of these two factors: the increasing rational incoherence of modern moral values and ideals, and their consequent increasing practical inadequacy for the purpose of regulating—orienting and giving meaning to— everyday life. (Bernstein, p. 5)

We can argue that the failures of modernity are caused by its failure to move beyond identitarian thinking. Modernity has failed in the promise of liberation and its highest values or ethical ideals have become suspect because they are tainted by wrong life. I will return to the problem of identitarian thinking in a moment.

So far, I have written about wrong life quite a bit without clearly defining it. At the very end of aphorism 18 in *Minima Moralia*, Adorno states, "wrong life cannot be lived rightly" (2005, p. 39). From our earlier analysis, we can conclude that, for Adorno, moral concepts are guides for life. They help us orient ourselves in the world and coordinate our activities and desires so that everyone will have freedom from fear and hunger, and have liberty with regard to self-development and self-determination. However, these moral concepts or principles must be employed under real social and historical conditions. If the historical and social conditions under which these concepts are to be employed are oppressive and dehumanizing, then such concepts lose their meaning and worth.

The employment of such concepts may even perpetuate oppression. Remember Marcuse's critique of repressive tolerance; under oppressive social conditions, tolerance, justice, and other moral concepts may have an effect that is the opposite of their intended use. Wrong life is a social situation where great inequalities in the necessary resources for self-development and self-determination give some social groups an advantage over others. Further, it is a situation where some groups suffer from various forms of discrimination and disrespect because of their social group membership. The problem is that, while the mechanisms that produce and reproduce social inequalities and disrespect are in full force, we still expect universal moral principles to apply equally to all.

Consider this example. Several years ago when I lived in Philadelphia, all of the candidates for Mayor presented the citizens of the city with their plans to curb violence. Most of the proposals embodied some kind of "getting tough on crime" policy. Many of the candidates thought that they could deal with the problem by putting more police officers on the streets, especially in particular areas. Not one candidate addressed the social conditions under which people lived in communities with high crime rates. No one talked about the importance of education or adequate resources. None of them talked about the poverty level in these communities. To address the issue of poverty would require a critique of the system that produces these impoverished pockets of our society. No one addressed the issue of wrong life, a wrong life that these unfortunate citizens are forced to live. Each of the proposals by the Mayoral candidates can be summed up as follows: "We know that you are poor, uneducated, mistreated, disrespected, and dehumanized, but be good."

These ideas return us to the issue of identitarian thinking, which has a leveling effect that smoothes over social contradictions. This is one of the key themes in Marcuse's *One-Dimensional Man* (1966). Contradictions are smoothed over so that real social inequalities are not recognized as such. All human beings are viewed as the same regardless of their radically different situations in life. Individuals are expected to live right in the context of wrong life. Wrong life is a social configuration where people are denied adequate resources for self-development and self-determination, they are exploited, for the gains of others, disrespected etc., and are still expected to uphold the moral norms and values of those who benefit from this unjust configuration.

4. Ideal Theory, Non-Ideal Theory, and the Veil of Injustice

Social and political theories that have attempted to offer us a means of escaping wrong life are plentiful. One of the grandest attempts was made by John Rawls. In this section, I will show how wrong life produces wrong theory even for those with good intentions. Let me say at the outset that I take the intent of Rawls's theory to be more radical than most people on the left give him credit for. Rawls's theory requires critical analyses of the basic structure of society. This critical analysis reveals that the basic structure of society tends toward injustice, unfairness, and inequality. Such a basic structure can only produce wrong life. Rawls is aware that, if the basic structure of society is built on principles that are not just and fair, there is no point in talking about individual morality. Therefore, according to Rawls, we must change the basic structure so that it conforms to principles of justice that are derived from a subject position of neutrality.

This critique of the basic structure of society may be the common ground between Rawls and Adorno. We may think of the basic structure of society, or to what Adorno refers as the totality, as a set of beliefs and values that undermine (or enhance) our ability to create a fair and just society. Almost everything taken up by this structure, if it is unjust, gets corrupted. In Lecture Seven of *History and Freedom* (2006), Adorno examines the enlightenment as well as the Hegelian views of the unfolding of reason. He writes:

> Thus we may speak of the irrationality of the *ratio* in the present historical phase; we may point out that the prodigious achievements of science benefit only a small group of people or that science seems to be moving towards the destruction of the human race. We may accuse reason of all sorts of other irrationalities. Indeed, I would not defend reason against these accusations; I would certainly not deny that, as the process of rationalization advances, it claims any number of victims. But we should not let things get out of proportion; we must be clear in our minds that the responsibility for the threats that the advancing sciences unleash on mankind lies not with reason or science, but with the way in which reason is *entwined* with very real social conditions. Within these social conditions reason is directed at purposes that are irrational because of the irrational state of society as a whole. (Ibid., p. 62)

Adorno's point is that scientific reason in itself is not bad or destructive and can be of great benefit to humanity. However, scientific reason unfolds within a particular socio-historical context. The dominant values in this social/historical context determine the way in which reason is employed. In the context of wrong life the rational becomes irrational and the irrational becomes rational. If reason is reduced to its instrumental function, it may become nothing more than a tool for the domination of nature and humanity. The totality that Adorno mentions, and the basic structure that Rawls talks about, is the totality of values that determine what use we make of reason and all of the moral concepts that flow from practical reason, especially with regard to their effects on people and the conditions of their existence.

My position here is that the goal of Rawls's theory is not the problem. The problem is with the method he suggests for arriving at our principles of justice. With good intention, Rawls constructs a method that requires complete impartiality. But this is the problem. Rawls's method requires that we hypothetically go under a veil of ignorance; our identity or particularity must undergo erasure. Only as disembodied consciousness are we capable of arriving at principles of justice that are not tainted by personal prejudice. Rawls's theory is tainted by what Adorno calls "identity thinking." The loss of the particular identity of every individual is at the same time the claim to one single identity. We are all human. We are all the same underneath our skin.

As Charles W. Mills has pointed out, this type of theory applies to an ideal world and not the world that we live in with its history of violence, racism, sexism, homophobia, and greed (Mills and Pateman, 2007). To this ideal theory, Mills opposes a non-ideal theory, which must not ignore but rather consider historical practices of injustice. Wrong life has real material consequences, which must be considered when trying to create a just society. The Rawlsian veil of ignorance is really a veil of injustice, since it requires that we forget the scars of injustice that some of us wear, scars that cannot be removed by any hypothetical erasure of identity. If life is to be lived rightly, then wrong life must not be concealed but made visible.

5. Conclusion

Mills's notion of non-ideal theory bears a resemblance to Adorno's negative dialectics. The ideal theory of Rawls aims at elucidating principles of justice in an ideal society. Since the society in which we live has a history of oppression of various sorts, an ideal theory cannot help us create a fair and just society. In our society corrective measures must be taken in light of damage done by systems of oppression. According to Mills, Rawls's theory is a sketching of rights, when what we actually need is a righting of wrongs (Mills and Pateman, 2008, p. 114), or, in the context of Adorno's work, the transformation of wrong life. Adorno's project represents an attempt to move us beyond formalism in ethics.

For Mills, Adorno, and Marcuse, social justice requires a transformation of our society, which must begin with an examination of the real social and historical mechanisms of oppression and then continue with a refusal to endorse them. Here we can read Adorno's critique of identity thinking along with Marcuse's critique of one-dimensional thinking. Identity thinking and one-dimensional thinking are attempts to smooth over social contradictions that are produced and maintained by oppressive, repressive, wrong life.

A conception of justice that views everyone as the same, in a society where gross inequalities exist, contributes to the smoothing over of these contradictions and perpetuates wrong life. Only recognition of real socially-constituted differences and the disadvantages created by them for the least of these in our society will make it possible to talk about and achieve concrete justice. Social and political philosophy must become liberation philosophy with its preferential treatment of least of these.

Four

INTERSECTIONALITY AND LOVE

Andrew Fitz-Gibbon

1. Introduction

This chapter arises out of a larger project in moral philosophy with a working title, *Love as a Guide to Morals*. My task is to examine love as a sufficient basis for moral life. In this paper, I address one facet of the larger moral picture: the important critical framework of intersectionality as a means of understanding layers of domination and oppression that contribute to human suffering. My suggestion is that intersectionality, as theoretically descriptive, alone does not provide a normative approach to human relationships. It needs a way of thinking about how normative moral commitments are shaped. My assertion is that love provides a useful compass to steer through the complexities of this particular moral maze.

Moral philosophers since David Hume have grappled with the difficult relationship between the empirically descriptive and the morally prescriptive. Hume's analysis has become known as "Hume's Law," "Hume's Guillotine" (Black 1969, p. 100), or the is/ought question (1969, p. 421). His assertion was that it is impossible to derive "ought statements" from "is statements." What is the case will never tell us what ought to be the case. Theoretical, sociological, political, and critical analyses, though so important in helping us understand what is actually true rather than what merely seems true, are indispensable. However, alone it cannot move us to moral commitments without some way of forming value judgments.

Hume thought that values derive from the innate human sympathy people have for others and from common sense benevolence. In contradistinction to Immanuel Kant, he argued that moral commitments couldn't be rationally justified. Hume established a trajectory in moral philosophy that would have profound influence in the twentieth century. George Edward Moore, building on Hume, likewise rejected any rational defense of morality and preferred an intuitive basis (1905).

In the early to mid-twentieth century, the trend continued. Many agreed with Hume and Moore—that morality had no rational basis—yet rejected both intuitionism and innate sympathy. All that was left of the moral project was emotivism: moral statements are merely expressions of emotion and have no truth-value. If this Humean trajectory is true, then all we can say morally about the oppression of which intersectionality theory speaks is that, "We do not like to be oppressed." It is mere expression of personal preference.

Not all moral philosophy took the emotivist turn, and emotivism has been critiqued well from a variety of perspectives: utilitarianism, neo-Kantianism, and renewed Aristotelianism, among others—perhaps Alasdair MacIntyre's *After Virtue* (1981) is the most important. The critique of emotivism need not delay us. However, the is/ought problem needs more careful attention, as it is that part of the Humean trajectory in ethics that will not go away.

William Donald Hudson edited a useful collection of essays on Hume's is/ought question (1969). These range from papers that support the understanding of Hume I have suggested above, to those that critique it, either disagreeing with Hume or disagreeing with the standard interpretation of Hume. In this chapter, I suggest a fivefold pathway through the difficulties of Hume's Law, with particular emphasis on love as normative for ethics. I then apply my findings to intersectionality theory.

2. Intersectionality as an Accurate Framework to Understand the Complexity of Oppression

Intersectionality is a comparatively new word used to describe the ways that socially or culturally constructed identities form a complex web of inequality. The concept was in use before the word was coined—first used by Kimberlé Crenshaw (1991)—and is rooted in the writings of black feminists from the early 1980s onward (Davis, 1981; Collins, 1990; James, 1998). Kathryn Russell has argued that the concept goes as far back as Karl Marx, who advanced an understanding of intersectionality in his methodology of abstraction and theory of internal relations, though it was not fully developed in his writings (2007). In brief, oppressive structures of society—gender, race, sexual orientation, nationality, ethnicity, class, and disability—do not operate in isolation, but form an intricate "Matrix of Domination" at the intersection of the various forms of oppression (Collins 1990, p. 225).

Black feminists gave voice to this idea when they realized that the issues of white middle-class women were not the same as for black working class women. For example, Angela Davis viewed the incipient racism of many white women feminists as equally oppressive as the sexism of patriarchal culture (1981, pp. 70ff.). This was also true of capitalism as oppressive of poor women (1981, pp. 149ff; see also, James, pp.129ff, pp.161ff).

To categorize a woman as female in a patriarchal culture did not sufficiently explain the experience of many women. Race, sexual orientation, and class also informed those socially constructed identities. Further, those who are oppressed in one identity, say "woman," can be at the same time an oppressor in another identity, say "white." A black woman in the United States might be considered oppressed in her cultural context, yet as a citizen of the United States, could be considered an oppressor to women in developing countries (Collins 1990, pp. 245–246). More recently, intersectionality has affected other areas of critical theory, including post-colonial discourse, queer theory, and Ecofeminism, where a similar conceptual framework has helped shed light on the experience of oppression.

Intersectionality theory has provided a framework for resistance. For example, to resist patriarchy, when patriarchy is allied to the dominating structures of capitalism that are allied to the oppressive structures of racism, is not sufficient. Resistance to one must be resistance to all.

However, it is unclear whether to resist is to resist the notion of categorization itself (the categories of race, gender, and class being problematic) or to resist the inequalities of society that the categories give expression to. Despite its complexity and the internal debate about what resistance to dominating categories means, intersectionality theory remains a useful and powerful tool to explain the condition of suffering for many women (as well as poor men of color and people with disabilities).

Yet, intersectionality theory shares the same conceptual difficulty with other theories that try to explain what is the case, and to move from that to what ought to be the case. Here I return to Hume's Law. Intersectionality theory itself does not clearly explain why, given the layering of oppression from multiple identities, that oppression *ought* to be resisted. The "nature of things," even when we have correctly described them—and I agree that intersectionality theory is a plausible explanation of oppression—tells us nothing about what should be the case.

In logic, we can only arrive at a prescriptive conclusion such as, "oppression should be resisted," when at least one prescriptive premise is in the argument. The moral philosophical task is to add—or uncover—that prescriptive premise to the argument. Even then, if a valid argument can be made, its soundness will depend on the quality and veracity of the prescriptive premise. It is the moral philosopher's task to provide a justification for just such a prescription.

3. Bridging the Is/Ought Gap

In my larger project, I argue that love is just such a sufficient guide to morals and that it provides a prescriptive premise for a valid moral argument. In the case of intersectionality theory, in response to the question, "Why resist the oppression of domination?" I answer, "Because that is the most loving thing to do."

However, I need to return to the is/ought question and a further consideration of love and "oughtness." I make a fivefold argument:

(1) A Humean naturalistic argument. I turn Hume's argument back upon himself. Hume was quite clear that "is" can never tell us what "ought" should be. It is a point of logic. However, it did not leave Hume with a moral vacuum. Hume was the model of civility and courteousness. He rooted morality not in an "ought to" but in the natural human feeling of sympathy (1969, p. 628). Nature leads people to be kind to others. In an-

other place, Hume favors benevolence, which he sees as equally natural to the human species (2006, p. 10). So, for Hume the answer to the is/ought dilemma is no dilemma at all. He simply removed "ought" and made morality (as sympathy or benevolence) part of what "is." I would modify Hume's naturalism and suggest that love is as innate to human beings as sympathy or benevolence. Benevolence is one of the effects of love (see below).

(2) An argument from perfection. Here I follow Iris Murdoch, who makes the case that, in contemplation of the good, we intuit what we ought to do. She makes something like a Platonic argument—something like, because she is not sure that the transcendent exists. She argues that by thinking about the perfect we are drawn to what should be (1970, chap. 1). She hints that love is the good (ibid., p. 45). By contemplating on the perfection of love, it is possible to know what we ought to do (see, Antonaccio, 2000, pp. 130ff).

(3) An elective teleological argument. Aristotle assumes that all things have a natural *telos*—a goal or purpose. The acorn has the *telos* of an oak tree. In natural terms, this makes sense only if the *telos* is organic, determined by nature itself. The acorn has no choice in the matter. If it grows, and nothing impedes its growth, it will become an oak tree. It could never become a cherry tree, or a pig. When this principle is applied to human life, the analogy with nature fails, unless one is a strict determinist. I take it that the idea of human choice has meaning. Where the acorn has no choice but to become an oak tree, the human subject has a choice in framing a purpose. I can choose a goal or purpose for my life. This I call "elective teleology." Through thought, dialogue, reading, and experience, I may choose one *telos* over another. In the larger project, I suggest that to choose love as the *telos* is worthy of consideration.

(4) An "if, then should" Kantian hypothetical imperative. Kant argued that two kinds of imperatives (commands) exist. Hypothetical imperatives are those that "represent the practical necessity of a possible action as a means for attaining something else that one wants" (1994, p. 24). A categorical imperative "would be one that represented an action as objectively necessary in itself, without reference to another end (ibid., p. 25). Kant was convinced that reason would lead us to categorical imperatives. For my part, I am not sure on two counts: (1) reason can do the task; and (2) categorical imperatives do exist. However, I feel on much safer ground with hypothetical imperatives. These take the form of "if, then should." For example, "If you want a good job after college, then you should work hard at your studies." The hypothetical imperative depends on defining the "if." In terms of elective teleology, the "if" is the chosen goal.

For classical Aristotelianism, if we would enjoy the eudemonistic life—ethical doctrine holding that the value of moral action lies in its capacity to produce happiness—, then we ought to pursue those things that make for *eudaimonia* (happiness). In my terms, if we want the good of love, then we should engage in the practice of love.

(5) Utilitarianism with love as the *summum bonum* (highest good). I take the genius of utilitarianism to be the distinction between the "good" and the "right." The right is always to seek to maximize that which is considered the good. In classical utilitarianism (hedonistic utilitarianism), pleasure is the good to be maximized as the right thing to do. A modified form would be to find the *summum bonum* in happiness (eudemonistic utilitarianism). This would be akin to Aristotelianism with its *telos* of *eudaimonia*. Joseph Fletcher suggested love as the *summum bonum* in what I would call "agapistic utilitarianism." The right thing to do is always to seek to maximize the utility of love in any situation. We should choose that course of action that will produce the most loving outcomes. For Fletcher, love is the same as benevolence (1966, pp. 60ff).

4. Love as a Sufficient Guide to Morals

Do I view love in the same way as Fletcher does? I do so in part. However, I do not take a monovalent approach to understanding love, as love is a complex human (more broadly, mammalian) experience. I suggest elsewhere in the larger project of which this chapter is a part that we can identify four ways of loving: erosic love, friendship, affection, and agapic love.

The order of these ways of loving is important as they form what I call "expanding circles of loving concern." Each broadens loving concern for the Other, from the most exclusive in erosic love, to the few in friendship—as conceived by Aristotle and others in that tradition of friendship—to the many in affection, to the most universal in agapic love.

I choose to keep two Greek descriptors because neither erosic nor agapic love easily translates into a single English word. Erosic love, for example, includes, among other ideas, sexual love, romance, and a non-sexual eros in the Platonic sense. Each way of loving is rooted in desire for the Other and involves movement from the self to the Other. Love as craving or desire I have borrowed from Augustine of Hippo, who modified Plato (Arendt 1996, p. 6). Love as movement toward the Other—the object of love—I have borrowed from Thomas Aquinas, though I use the notion of movement in a metaphorical rather than metaphysical way (*Summa Theologicae* 2.1.26). Love as movement from the self, an "unselfing," I have borrowed from Murdoch (see Ruokonen, 2002, pp. 211–213).

This movement from the self to the Other contains four moral effects of love. I am tempted to call these effects "Works of Love," following Søren

Kierkegaard (1847). His reason was to distinguish love as deed from love as merely feeling, and his reason seems a good one. If it were the case that by the mid-nineteenth-century love was often understood in only romantic or sentimental ways—sentimental in either its popular cultural sense or technical ethical sense following Hume—then it is much more the case now. Love in a moral sense makes ethical demands. Love commands. To make a distinction between love as feeling and love as choice is helpful, and Kierkegaard led the way. However, his error, and he is not alone, was to remove moral love so far from sentimental love that we have difficulty seeing how the two may both be called love. For love to be a guide to morals we must deal with love in all its marvelous complexity and ambiguity. That will include a discussion of how erosic love, friendship, and affection may guide morals without relegating them to sentimentality, and hence, to moral irrelevance.

What are the four moral effects of love?

(1) Love seeks the good of the Other. This is the general moral principle of beneficence. Love—whether erosic, friendship, affection or agapic—works for the good of the loved one.

(2) Love seeks never to harm the Other. This is the general moral principle of non-maleficence and is the accompaniment to beneficence. To do good and to do no harm are the moral implications of love (despite popular song, "You Always Hurt the Ones You Love," Roberts and Fisher, 1944).

(3) Love respects the personhood and integrity of the Other. The Other is a person in their own right with all the responsibilities and rights of an autonomous individual.

(4) Love works toward justice for the Other. Of course, this depends on what is meant by justice. A Rawlsean "justice as fairness" position (1971) would be a useful place to start and provides at least a beginning conversation.

Taking these effects of love and integrating them into my "circles of loving concern" approach, love as a guide to morals would seek good and not harm for the Other. Also, love would respect the personhood and work for justice for the Other—be the Other erosic lover, friend, family member, or stranger. The intensity of that loving concern is strongest closest to the center circle. Loving concern is stronger and more demanding with proximity. For example, a parent would show greater loving concern for her child than for a child who lives in some distant land.

Love makes a cosmopolitan demand—love of the neighbor must mean love for all—yet the requirements of love lessen with distance. This position steers a middle course between the ethicists of care who assert that no universal requirement to care for all esists, and Peter Singer's rigorous utilitarianism (2000, pp. 118 ff.) or Kwame Anthony Appiah's cosmopolitanism (2006, p. xiii), where each counts as only one and where every one is in the same relationship to every other one. My position is a modified universalism.

5. Intersectionality and Love

What has love to do with intersectionality? I make two suggestions: (1) love is an adequate and sufficient prescriptive basis for a moral response to the fact of oppression that intersectionality names; (2) love, as a moral response, moves beyond resistance toward transformed relationships that affect both oppressed and oppressor.

First, love, as a guide to morals, gives to intersectionality theory what it lacks as a merely descriptive critical theory. It provides intersectionality theory with a reason why oppression, in its many layers, is morally wrong. Oppression is a failure to love. Oppression fails the test of seeking good, doing no harm, respecting the Other, and seeking the Other's justice. Love provides intersectionality theory with a normative moral language for what should and should not to be the case.

Second, the moral response of love affects oppressor and oppressed alike. Intersectionality theory requires the oppressed to resist the oppressors; to take destiny into their own hands. Intersectionality theory assumes that the one who causes suffering cannot change. Yet, love requires of the oppressor loving action, too, on behalf of those oppressed. In the transformation of love, the oppressor ceases to be such. Further, and this is more contentious, love moves beyond resistance to seek goodness and justice for the oppressor too. Love works toward loving community.

In conclusion, returning to Murdoch's perfectionism, for intersectionality theory, the possibility exists to imagine the perfect world, where no forms of oppression exist. The social roles and self-identities people assume would not make for a web of oppression, but a web of fulfillment, well-being, and goodness, where no one would be harmed and all would be respected, where justice would be done.

In my terms, such would be a loving community. The perfect draws us toward itself.

Five

MORAL CONVICTION AND DISAGREEMENT: GETTING BEYOND NEGATIVE TOLERATION

Matthew Pianalto

He moves in darkness as it seems to me
Not of woods only and the shade of trees.
He will not go behind his father's saying,
And he likes having thought of it so well
He says again, "Good fences make good neighbors."
　　　　　— Robert Frost, "Mending Wall" (1915, pp. 12–13)

1. Introduction

Toleration appears to be essential for peace in any sufficiently diverse society. At the same time, no one thinks that we should (or can) tolerate everything. That limits exist to what is tolerable gives rise to a difficult puzzle to be resolved by any society in which some of the differences between individuals or groups are, or seem to be, differences in their moral convictions.

The puzzle can be illustrated as follows. Suppose that a friend of mine has a strong moral conviction that abortions are seriously morally wrong. She knows that others disagree with her, but the fact of disagreement does not weaken her conviction, and because this is a *moral*, rather than a merely personal conviction (or commitment), she judges that abortion is ipso facto intolerable. We can reason that if *anything* is intolerable, actions that are seriously morally wrong would be intolerable, and so, suggesting that my friend should, nevertheless, tolerate the practice of providing and obtaining abortions, would appear to be odd.

The problem with demanding toleration of acts and practices judged to be deeply immoral is that it calls upon individuals to exercise restraint or forbearance in a case where they judge that quite the opposite attitudes and actions are called for. To tolerate what we find deeply immoral would appear to require that we not act in accord with our moral convictions. Thus, practicing toleration in such cases would involve a compromise of our moral integrity. Tolerating what we find deeply immoral would require that we act in a way discordant with our deepest moral convictions.

Nevertheless, where moral disputes result from differences in worldview or way of life, on matters where reasonable people can disagree, defenders of a liberal society will often hold that we must tolerate such differences, even when they cut against our own moral convictions. But if abiding by the demand for toleration sometimes results in a compromise of integrity, then practicing toleration will tend to alienate people from their moral convictions. (Here I borrow the language Williams (1963) used to criticize the alienating effects of utilitarian thinking.)

Some might say, "so much the worse for moral convictions." But in what follows, I will try to illustrate why that is the wrong response, and to show how toleration and moral conviction aren't necessarily opposed. It is possible to preserve moral integrity while at the same time practicing a form of toleration toward those with whom we have considerably deep moral disagreements. Importantly, if toleration is to be compatible with integrity, it must be something more than a mere "putting up with" the fact of moral disagreement. Indeed, this is the kind of negative construal of toleration that gives rise to the problem of alienation.

2. Why Toleration?

The difficulty sketched above might appear to present a false dilemma. Perhaps we have no need to call for toleration in cases of moral disagreement. Instead, what we need is, say, "civil intolerance." If my friend believes that abortion is seriously morally wrong, then she should join an anti-abortion group, spend her weekends peacefully demonstrating at abortion clinics, and, if she has the requisite political genius, get involved with anti-abortion lobbying efforts. At no point need she express any toleration toward a practice she finds morally deplorable, and all of her protest and lobbying activities are, if anything, going to be an expression of her intolerance. Furthermore, these ways of registering her view that abortion is intolerable would constitute precisely the sort of activities by which she can act with integrity (consistent with her convictions), while still recognizing the value of peace and civility.

This response to the problem posed above suggests that toleration is not as essential to a peaceful society as is a basic commitment to conducting oneself peacefully even in the face of moral disagreement. However, a genuine commitment to civil intolerance may, at times, require that we act with restraint and forbearance; such a commitment would limit the sorts of actions and exercises of power that we could legitimately employ against those with whom we has deep moral disagreements.

We can express this point in the language of toleration by pointing out that a serious commitment to dealing civilly with the moral disagreements we have with others still requires some minimum amount of toleration. At a minimum, we have to tolerate their existence enough that we do not violate our commitment to finding a peaceful way either of altering their beliefs or stopping their practices. Following Hans Oberdiek, we might classify this sort of toleration under either what he calls "bare toleration," which "acknowledges the desirability of not coming to blows with people who must live together," or "mere toleration," in which we simply respond to those we think are living badly, "it's their funeral" (2000, pp. 28–30).

Oberdiek, however, points out that these forms of toleration work best— at least, best achieves their (superficial) form of peace—when those who must be tolerated can be largely ignored or made invisible. We can "put up with" differences we find disagreeable when they do not invade our lives in any significant way. But of course, in the example I began with, the conviction that others are doing something seriously morally wrong *does* invade my friend's life—the practices of others are an affront to what she finds morally acceptable. Given this, I might insult her moral seriousness to say that even though she deeply disapproves of what others do, she must manifest at least some minimal (bare) level of toleration toward such people. On the other hand, the prospects for her acts of civil intolerance having any significant impact look grim. For example, if she found herself in a minority, and politically weak, position on the issue, then pointing out her right to such displays of civil intolerance may seem like a mere consolation prize.

The basic difficulty here, whether we paint the picture in terms of civil intolerance or bare toleration, is that the resulting community of moral agents is not much of a community at all. Deep disagreements and power struggles about fundamental moral ideals—struggles that have only the superficial quality of civility in that they do not involve *physical* conflict—may persist. The bare commitment to peace and civility is little more than a *modus vivendi*, and, because of this, a distinct risk of alienation and moral frustration arises.

Under these conditions, unfortunately, some *will* ultimately take moral matters into their own hands, as Scott Roeder did with George Tiller. Tiller was a controversial doctor who provided late-term abortions; Roeder shot Tiller dead in the lobby of Tiller's church on 31 May 2009 (Joe Stumpe and Monica Davey, "Abortion Doctor Shot to Death in Kansas Church," *New York Times*, 1 June 2009). While we might chalk such actions up to the instability of such individuals, they reflect, in my view, the instability that John Rawls identified in any society in the condition of a *modus vivendi* (2005, pp. 146–147). As in Robert Frost's "Mending Wall," if we think of bare toleration as an intellectual fence that separates those on each side, it is far from clear that very much of it makes for good neighbors, rather than for total (moral) strangers.

In the remainder of this paper, I will suggest that a solution to this difficulty can be located by reworking the grounds for toleration and by construing toleration as a process that is not merely negative—one that involves more than simply putting up with difference. In addition, I will elucidate that this process is, itself, integrity-preserving, and may strengthen (or deepen) our integrity in ways that merely staying on our own side of the fence cannot.

3. Beyond Negative Toleration to Tolerant Engagement

Toleration, construed as the negative activity of restraint and forbearance, may preserve kind of peace between disagreeing parties. However, in addition to the fact that such disagreeing parties remain, at bottom, adversaries, significant problems concerning justice in a "negatively tolerant" society also remain. Two related difficulties, which I will only point to here, arise when an imbalance in power between conflicting parties exists, since the stronger party can honor the duty to tolerate either by disregarding the other party or, when the stronger abhors some belief or practice of the other party, by arranging matters so that the voice of the weaker party can have no significant effect on public discussion or policy. Tolerating a person's views—if tolerating is merely putting up with—does not require that we allow their views to receive, for example, a public hearing. If we believe that their views are seriously morally misguided, we have all the more reason to use our power to ensure that the weaker party is not taken seriously by others. Robert Paul Wolff, Herbert Marcuse, and, more recently, Wendy Brown, have critiqued toleration that takes these forms, insofar as "toleration" often turns out to be a smokescreen for the protection of the status quo (Wolff and Marcuse, 1969; Brown, 2006).

Such responses to disagreement are problematic because the form of toleration at work here allows, where it does not actually encourage, minimal engagement with other members of one's community. Minimal, and often adversarial, engagement is probably not the best recipe for mutual understanding. As Barbara Herman suggests, it is unlikely to provide a sound framework for developing a "community of moral judgment"—which shares positive ideals—out of those who see themselves as having fundamental moral disagreements with others in the community (1996). Call this the "problem of insulation": if we only tolerate others by putting up with their differences or, where we can't abide by that, engaging in civil intolerance (which still requires the degree of toleration necessary to preserve peace), we run the risk of insulating ourselves from these others, of excluding them from our sense of the community.

The problem of insulation arises when we consider our moral disagreements only from the standpoint of our own moral perspective. Of course, that is both a natural and an important standpoint from which to view them. But it is important to notice that, in tolerating something, we must have some understanding of what we are tolerating before we can even judge whether it *is* to be tolerated, and to what extent. We cannot make a fully informed judgment here unless we have some understanding of the perspective of the others with whom we disagree. That is not something we can learn from our own perspective. Thus, toleration—or more precisely, *moral* toleration—cannot be thought of as merely an activity of restraint and forbearance, but also requires active engagement, which aims at a sympathetic understanding of the other. Because we often judge prior to understanding the other's perspective, the cultivation of a proper amount of toleration (or intolerance) requires more than merely settling the matter from our own perspective. It requires, instead, what I call "tolerant engagement."

We might object that a principle that holds that we must tolerantly engage with those with whom we have serious moral disagreements is just as potentially alienating as any other principle of toleration. "Alienating," however, is not the right word here. It might be uncomfortable, surprising, and frustrating, but tolerantly engaging with others, just as with any principle of toleration, does not force *acceptance* on anyone. Of course, acceptance, agreement, and resolution may result, and some might fear that such results would involve a loss of one's own integrity insofar as any of those results would imply some adjustment to our own original convictions.

Part of the response to such a worry is that integrity does not demand rigidity at all costs. If it did, then persons of integrity would be the sorts of persons who never grew intellectually or made adjustments in their views. However, we have no reason to think that considered adjustments and revisions to our views mean that we have suddenly lost our integrity. Our convictions are valuable for the guidance and framework they provide in our lives. They do not have some further, intrinsic value just because they are *our* convictions. As Gabriele Taylor puts it, "should the occasion arise [the person of integrity] will be capable of self-criticism" (1987, p. 158; see also Davion, 1991).

The principle that we should tolerantly engage with others with whom we have moral disagreements flows from both the virtue of humility and the principle of respect for persons. The need for humility flows from the recognition that regardless how right we think we are, we are, after all, only human and not infallible beings. Cultivating humility need not lead us to abandon our convictions, but it does rule out the kinds of dogmatism and self-righteousness that would perpetuate the problem of insulation.

At the same time, as Karl Popper explains, acknowledging our fallibility also need not lead us to embrace relativism (1987). For Popper, humility (and thereby, tolerance) undergirds the search for truth, and, given the possibility of error, humility enables us to avoid insulation that would be counterproductive to that search. On the other hand, respect for persons requires that we see others *as* persons and, where we have moral disagreements, as persons who may (for all we know) have their own considered reasons for their practices. Aiming toward a sympathetic understanding of others is a way of practicing such respect and of humbly acknowledging our own non-ideal situation as knowers and believers.

4. Forms of Tolerant Engagement

Tolerant engagement can take on various forms in practice. Importantly, tolerant engagement is an integrity-preserving, rather than an integrity-compromising activity. Cultivating moral integrity is not only, as Cheshire Calhoun points out, simply a matter of "sticking to our guns," but also involves developing a well-grounded understanding of our convictions and of the moral terrain they cover (1995, p. 259). Tolerant engagement contributes to this process insofar as it encourages sympathetic, rather than adversarial, interaction with those with whom we have moral disagreements. The point is that we don't know what we can learn from others until we make an honest attempt to learn *from* them, rather than simply *about* them.

The most straightforward form of tolerant engagement is *discourse*. In discourse, we share our views with others, seeking to make our views and the reasons for them, intelligible to others, who do not share them. Importantly, discourse should be distinguished from *debate*, which, because it is essentially adversarial, is a zero-sum activity. Debaters seek to win the debate in the eyes of an *audience*, not necessarily to make themselves intelligible to the other debater. Discourse, on the other hand, leaves open the possibility of deeper understanding and a shifting in focal points from which we view those with whom we disagree—learning *from*, rather than merely about, them. There is no guarantee that discourse will lead to *full* understanding or agreement, but even where this does not occur, it is to be hoped that tolerant discourse can allow us to keep in view the humanity of those with whom we have moral disagreements, and will provide a space in which we can sympathetically look for other common ground.

Another form engagement can take is *compromise*. It may seem odd to speak of compromise when moral convictions are at stake, since moral convictions would seem to be the very things on which we cannot coherently compromise. Sometimes, however, conflicting members of communities must make practical (or policy) decisions about morally charged matters, as discussed, for example, by Mary Warnock (1987). We need to distinguish between compromising our convictions or integrity and making procedural compromises in the interests of policy.

Importantly, engaging in a policy-making process would not require persons to abandon their basic convictions, even if we knew (or suspected) that our convictions would probably not be fully matched by the resulting policy. We can always vote against the final proposal. In addition, making compromises can lead to a better result from the standpoint of our convictions than simply sitting out the meeting.

We do risk that the trade-offs involved in compromise will be adversarial, but where policy debates are informed by the ideal of tolerant engagement and sympathetic discourse, the possibility exists for those with strong convictions to allow pragmatic compromises in the interest of developing a policy that aligns as closely as possible to their actual convictions.

Maintaining our integrity doesn't require that others come to agree with us, but it does, presumably, involve doing what we can to ensure that our voice is heard. The general points here are supported, and considered in careful detail, by Martin Benjamin in his work on compromise and integrity

(1990). Pragmatic compromise is an essential part of most political enterprises, but this sort of compromise should not be confused with, or equated to, a compromise of our convictions.

Finally, tolerant engagement can come in the form of *integration*. Pauline Graham explores this strategy in significant detail (1998). By contrast with compromise, where mutual concessions are made to secure some practical resolution (and which Graham construes as a primarily adversarial practice), integration occurs when conflicting parties move beyond their competing claims and identify a common problem they can solve collaboratively, despite their moral differences.

At first, how persons or groups with conflicting moral claims could possibly enter into this kind of engagement might not be immediately evident, since how to transform a conflict of values into a collective problem to be solved is unclear (aside, say, from the problem of maintaining peace between various groups). Nevertheless, some possibilities can be identified. Often, those with conflicting moral views can agree that other social problems exist that are related to their concerns. In the case of abortion, all may share concerns about rates of teenage pregnancy. In the case of the death penalty, all may be concerned with defects in the legal system that result in wrongful conviction and execution.

In such cases, those with conflicting moral convictions can agree on the importance of some kinds of projects in which members of both groups can participate and contribute. It may be unlikely that such integrated projects can themselves resolve moral disagreements, but the worthiness of such projects can encourage those with divergent convictions to see each other in a new light, possibly enhancing the tolerant attitudes conducive to further discourse on their points of conflict. Integration develops a positive relationship between the parties rooted in a common cause. At the same time, each person (or group) can engage in such integrated projects from the standpoint of their own convictions, and thus integration, too, requires no compromise of conviction or integrity.

5. The Limits of Tolerant Engagement

The difficult question is how far tolerant engagement can or should be taken. Some acts are *obviously* intolerable; for example, rape and child abuse. To question those cases would throw our moral competence into question (Lichtenberg, 1994). Equally, it would make little sense to seek tolerant engagement with people who advocate the obviously intolerable. While those points do not get us far, they are sufficient to elucidate the confusion of treating tolerance as an end in itself (as criticized by Marcuse, 1969, p. 82ff; see also). Indeed, if we are to think of *tolerance* as a virtue in an Aristotelian fashion, then the activity of this virtue must be located somewhere between inappropriate forms of *both* toleration *and* intoleration.

In that respect, intolerance is, in some contexts, the virtuous response. The civil intolerance, which I regarded with some suspicion above, may well be the correct response, but only when the possibilities of tolerant engagement have been genuinely exhausted. If we need a reminder of the forms virtuous intolerance can take, perhaps re-read Henry David Thoreau's "Civil Disobedience" (2008, pp. 276–300) and Martin Luther King, Jr.'s "Letter from Birmingham Jail" (1990, pp. 289–302).

However, both Thoreau and King were dealing with unjust institutions, and my discussion has focused on moral disagreements between individuals. Nevertheless, we can take from them the thought that tolerant engagement cannot occur if either party to the disagreement refuses to engage in this spirit. One difficulty here is that we may judge that genuine discourse, conducted in a spirit of truthfulness, is impossible with some person or group—Holocaust deniers, perhaps—and such people might, in turn, complain that we are failing to live up to our ideal of tolerant engagement. (Since I am discussing tolerance and toleration at the level of individuals, I will put aside for now the thorny question about the extent to which a society as a whole can or should tolerate the activities of such groups.) Here, not much can be said (in brief) except that we take certain things as signs that a person is deeply "out of touch with reality." Perhaps such people can be educated back into reality, perhaps not. But as Raimond Gaita suggests, the attempt to have a discussion with these sorts of people will only end up looking like a parody of discussion (2000, p. 158).

Thus, I hope I do not speak only for myself in suggesting that there is no deep reason to be alarmed philosophically by the sort of complaint mentioned above when it comes, say, from a Holocaust denier, who insists that we are not being tolerant if we refuse to discuss the evidence for and against this atrocity. If we are to discuss anything at all with each other, it must be something else.

Another difficulty is that discourse will often fail to produce agreement; one or both sides may simply come away feeling that what they understand better is why they think the other side is so wrong. As Chris Cowley (2005) has pointed out, the hope that clear-headed, rational discussion will ultimately lead to agreement may be misguided, and people with deep convictions may well feel insulted by the suggestion that they must simply "agree to disagree." We might still hope that discourse will allow those involved to see the humanity of those with whom they disagree, and the principle of respect for persons is certainly not void even when we judge that tolerant engagement is no longer a possibility.

I believe that sensible people can often, despite their own convictions, recognize that the contentious and complex nature of many moral issues can lead to disagreements that are not obviously unreasonable. We might think that sensible people would have no firm convictions about those issues. In my view, that is mistaken. The human spirit is large enough to contain within it convictions and humility. Nevertheless, persistent disagreements may threaten the possibility of a coherent community, and the very idea of a community presupposes some significant range of agreement in practice and belief. Therefore, the situation of heterogeneous societies is necessarily precarious, but not impossible.

I would suggest that the crucial aspect of this paper, for the sake of promoting discourse between disputing parties, is the thought that tolerant engagement is no threat to our integrity. Would it show greater integrity if we persistently shouted down our opponents in the manner of talking heads like Bill O'Reilly and Keith Olbermann? I fear that those who look to such personalities for truth rather than as sideshow entertainment are in serious danger of forgetting what genuine engagement with others is.

Indeed, because tolerant engagement is an expression (or enactment) of proper humility and respect for persons, it—like the virtues from which it flows—is a crucial element in a life of integrity, and is, thereby, a crucial ideal for maintaining the coherence of a community in the face of sometimes unavoidable disagreement. Where tolerant engagement succeeds, it not only maintains coherence (or peace), but also fosters moral and intellectual growth; whereas, the "negative toleration" critiqued above threatens to result in stagnation.

Six

IN SUPPORT OF THE GIRLS FROM 'ROUND HERE: BLACK FEMINIST REFLECTIONS ON THE UTILITY OF RAGE FOR BUILDING COMMUNITIES OF SUPPORT

V. Denise James

During the summer, I spend a few days each week writing in a coffee shop in downtown, Dayton, Ohio. The walk from my apartment takes me by the public transportation "bus hub." Given my propensity to get a late start, I often find myself navigating through a crowd of high-school students. Most of these kids are black and come from poor and working class families. Some of the kids are on their way to summer jobs and from summer school; so many more of them are just "hanging out."

Not so long ago, I was one of those kids, standing on Broad Street, in Richmond, Virginia. Broad Street socializing and waiting to be bussed to a school located across town from my home neighborhood.

During one of these walks to write, as I was reminiscing about the joy and freedom of that time hanging outside with my friends, I heard a loud voice: "Fuck you then, bitch" and saw a boy pulling the hand of a girl who was obviously attempting to ignore his advances. When she finally struggled free, her girlfriend ushered her through the group of teenage boys, who continued the verbal assault. I watched the two girls, heads held high against the battering, trying their best to ignore the curses and to appear unfazed.

I remembered that part of being outside too—the constant harassment, the fear, the chance that this might be the day I would have to fight or run, to face the stares as older people watched and offered no help. I found my adult-self enraged for the young girl I had been and for the two girls I did not know, but I was a step too late, too singular in the crowd in my anger to defend them in any successful way.

I arrived at the coffee shop angry—hopping mad, unable to work on the article this chapter was supposed to have been—unwilling to let the anger go. Something should be done. Had I not just gotten into an argument with an old man the day before on the same street when he said something lewd to me as I waited to cross? How could I spend my time writing about feminism and democracy theory when I knew intimately just how unsafe the urban streets were for black girls and women? I had to find a way to make my anger productive. I wanted to understand the relationships urban black women have to public spaces and how we might imagine a public space where we might be politically empowered and feel physically and mentally safe.

I am uncertain that a single solution to these issues exists, or whether the work necessary to make our communities more just can ever be completed in full. I am certain that every effort to work toward our ideals of justice is a necessary, worthwhile effort. I am certain because I am certain that the emotional and physical well-being of black women depends upon it.

These are reflections about the use of rage in relation to building communities of support and resistance. I contend that such communities offer the safety necessary for equality in the public sphere. The guarantee of personal safety is a condition for the possibility for individual autonomy and for the emergence of effective urban public spheres in communities across the United States. Rage and safety appear to be strange bedfellows, yet, with many other black feminists, I contend that the rage at the vulnerability of women and girls, as well as other socially oppressed people, is not an emotion we should repress. Instead, its extension into outrage against domination and violence is a first step to building inclusive community.

There are two moments of rage that may urge us to democratic action. The first is the rage at violation that we personally experience when we or others we care for are made unsafe. The rage at violation can be understood as an anger that occurs when our bodily safety and status as autonomous beings are violated. The second moment of rage can also be called outrage. We become outraged when we decide that the offense should not occur in our community. The moment of outrage is the extension of our feelings that our individual efforts at autonomous action should be extended to others whom we may or may not know personally. I contend that both rage and outrage can be creative emotions and do not have to result in violence.

In what follows, to frame my reflections, I begin by turning to Jody Miller's *Getting Played: African American Girls Urban Inequality and Violence* (2008), a sociological account of the sexual and gender-based harassment of young black women in an urban United States' city. I also consider the philosophies of rage and anger found in the works of black feminists Audre Lorde, bell hooks, and June Jordan. For all of them, the passionate resistance to sexism and racism is initiated and sustained by emotional disavowal of oppression and domination.

In 1981, during a climate of hostility between women of color feminists and their white peers, poet, activist, and scholar, Lorde told the National Women's Studies Association Conference, that instead of denying it, we should recognize, "anger is loaded with information and energy" (1984, p. 127). Fourteen years later, bell hooks returns to anger in her aptly titled and controversial book, *Killing Rage: Ending Racism.* hooks claims that she is not a victim and that instead, her rage "is a constructive healing rage" (1995, p. 18). If hooks and Lorde have much to offer us when we consider rage's utility for our anti-racist justice projects, then Jordan's 1996 keynote address to the

San Francisco Conference of the National Coalition against Sexual Assault helps us focus that utility on the subject at hand—violence against black women and girls. Thus, I rely heavily on her efforts in that address, "Notes toward a Model of Resistance," which highlights the "stunning energy of rage" against injustice and violation as the vital beginning of a response to the violence of rape and our efforts to build communities of resistance and support (2002).

Although I limit these deliberations exclusively to the experiences of urban United States black women from the poor and working class, the concerns expressed here could be extended to other women in other contexts because of shared experiences of oppression and gender based domination. I am also acutely aware that the social conditions of black men and women in the United States are intimately related and not easily distinguished analytically or practically. so, Therefore, my observations here have as much practical import for black men and boys as they do for the black girls and women I have made the focus of my analysis, a point that I will develop in the next section. Moreover, I believe that the claims I make here about rage and outrage in relation to building just, democratic communities may prove useful to anyone interested in such projects.

Miller's *Getting Played* is a sobering sociological study of the daily harassment many young girls face. Confirming the widespread occurrence of scenes like the one that occasioned this paper, Miller catalogues instances of domestic violence, sexual harassment in both the public spaces of neighborhoods and at school, and the high rates of exposure to crime experienced by the black teenage girls she studied in St. Louis, Missouri. Writing as a criminologist, Miller asserts, "violence against young women is a ubiquitous but too often invisible feature of the urban landscape, and it remains largely underexamined and thus undertheorized" (ibid., p.1).

According to Miller, criminology neglects violence and harassment against urban black girls in part because of the discipline's traditional masculinist viewpoint that causes it to only consider male subjects. Beyond that obvious point of neglect, Miller speculates that part of the reason why criminologists and others interested in urbanity and justice have not taken up the subject with more zeal is that violence against young black women is often perpetrated by young black men. Miller candidly writes about what she calls the "struggle" of writing about and researching this phenomenon because of what it may seem to imply about young black men:

> We do not need another reason to demonize poor minority young men. But since we know that most violence, including violence against women, is both intra-racial and involves similarly situated individuals often known to one another, this reticence has meant that we have neglected to understand the unique experiences and risks face by African American women and girls, particularly those in disadvantaged urban communities. (Ibid., p. 3)

The racist stereotyping that brands the young black male as dangerous is still alive and supported by the media and by local, state, and national policies, which profile all that is young and black and male as criminal. In the face of omnipresent racism, studies about violence committed by black men and perpetrated upon black women seem risky. Yet, as Miller's study argues, the issues of urban poverty and gender-based violence are urgent issues for the well being of young black girls. I would add that the issue is urgent not only for young black girls but also for young black men whose chances for well-being, individual safety, and choice are undermined when they become violent abusers.

We live in a society where the institutionalization and normalization of sexism and racism go hand in hand with the structural conditions of poverty and disenfranchisement that support the blight in and criminal economies of urban neighborhoods that limit the life chances and possibilities of young black men. The issue of gender-based harassment is both structural in a sense that exceeds the individual instances and intimate in a way that must be rallied against in the spaces of our homes and communities, even as the structural foundations of it remain.

June Jordan would find the root of our fears about articulating the rage occasioned by intra-racial, gender-based violence in our individual need for communities to support our resistance to oppression and our individual well-being. Many black feminist theorists and some black women, who cannot bear to call themselves feminists, have written with clarity about the primacy race identity has taken in their work and their lives over their gender-based concerns. On the one hand, black women have had a storied relationship to the exclusionary traditions of mainstream feminist movement and theory. On the other, black women have faced great resistance to their gendered concerns within the confines of traditional black political movements.

Articulating the intersecting nature of identities and oppression based on those identities has become a distinguishing characteristic of black feminist thought. Employing the fruits of these efforts into the consideration of personal safety, autonomy, and the prospects of community opens many doors to possible democratic projects.

In "Notes toward a Model of Resistance," June Jordan attempts to theorize a way that women can begin to respond to rape. She looks to the methods she and her students employed during protests against the 1996 California Proposition 209 against affirmative action as a model of such a response. She weds the feeling of accomplishment and freedom she had during the group protest to her estimation of her response to the violation of being raped. The insights of that exploration can also serve as models of equitable community building that would support the individual protection and flourishing of young black women. In "Notes," Jordan writes with astonishing lucidity and frankness about her experiences of being raped twice, first by a white acquaintance and then by a black man who happened to be the local president of the National Association for the Advancement of Colored People (NAACP). In her estimation of her reactions to the violations of each rape, Jordan writes:

> I mean it took me a while to notice that finally I could get to a "do or die" level of rage only by focusing upon the fact that he was a white man ordering me a black woman around. I could not reach my self-protective rage on any other basis: for example. On the basis of the fact that A Man was raping me, A Woman. . . . And I thought so then, and I think now there is a huge, known community out here working against racism and racist violence. But violence against women did not and does not have a remotely comparable huge and known community working against that pathology that saturates public consciousness, that pathology that depicts women and girls as troublesome idiots or unbearable bitches or uncontrollable whores or the Eve Root of all Evil. (2002, p. 79)

If she felt her response to her rape by a white man had been delayed, Jordan found herself unable to respond with self-protective rage against violation by a black man as well. Not only was shock generated by the violation she experienced, but also she felt as if she had no community context to give her psychological support during the rape. Neither did she have support during her recovery as a woman who had been violated. She recounts, "race paralyzed me to the extent of self-effacement" (ibid., p. 80). Elsewhere, she explains her longing for a feminist community as "seeking an attitude" that would make such a community of support for black girls and women possible (ibid., p. 95).

When Jordan considers the strides made by anti-racist movements, whose communities react with urgency when racism threatens its members, she asks the serious question, "Have we played too nice about gender based violence and dominance?" Perhaps, she offers, we have not yet gotten angry enough about sexism and harassment.

Rage and outrage are rarely considered as both appropriate reactions to violation and as prerequisites of resistance in our theoretical approaches to social problems. In our everyday lives, when we find ourselves confronted with the personal and social affronts of sexism, we do often respond with rage. We talk back, we shout, sometimes, we strike. Yet, our individual responses of rage seem inadequate. We do not want to promote attitudes and identities of rage as the key to solving women's problems. The productive force of rage is feared because it brings to mind violence. And we are tired of violence. The struggle for justice and equity is a stand against violence.

In her poems, speeches, and essays, Audre Lorde presents an interpretation of anti-racist anger and the difference between hatred and anger that avoids the sterility of many contemporary philosophies of the emotions by emphasizing the creative energy of anger. Accused by white feminists of being angry with them and hence, inhospitable to the possibilities of a unified feminist movement, Lorde argued that anger in itself was not a bad thing and that the goal should not be to get rid of the angry voices among feminists but to work against hatred. She wrote, "Hatred is the fury of those who do not share our goals, and its object is death and destruction. Anger is a grief of distortions between peers, and its object is change" (1984, p. 129).

Moreover, according to Lorde, "When we turn from anger we turn from insight, saying we will accept only the designs already known, deadly and safely familiar" (ibid., p. 131). In her diagnosis of the problems within the feminist movement, Lorde saw the fear of anger as a stumbling block to genuine coalition building. If white feminists could not or would not hear about the anger their racism occasioned in black women, then they could not be allies, because, for black women, the intersecting oppressions of race and gender could not be separated.

Lorde astutely considered how the internalization of hate felt by black women made them perpetuate racism and sexism even in their interactions with one another. In *Getting Played*, the girls often recounted the stories of the abuse of other women and girls with an ambivalence that illustrates the danger of such internalization (Miller, 2008). Writing about her often tense interactions with other black women and how quick she was to point out their failings, Lorde contended, that as a black woman, who from an early age faced the hate of racism and the ubiquity of sexism, she internalized those hatreds. She noted, "children know only themselves as reasons for the happenings in their lives. So, of course as a child I decided there must be something terribly wrong with me that inspired such contempt" (1984, p. 146). As she got older, she directed that contempt onto other black women. When we do not get outraged on behalf of others, we allow such a distortion to continue. We allow young girls to think that they "asked for it" when they are abused, or to think that other woman must have "had it coming."

bell hooks takes on the pathology of internalizing racism and suppressing rage in *Killing Rage*. hooks asserts that experiencing rage is not, in itself, inappropriate. She begins by recounting a personal experience during a flight, where, after a long day of being targeted for abuse because of her race, she sits down beside a white male passenger who refuses to acknowledge racism. hooks seethes. Following her narrative, we can imagine her sitting on the plane, angry that her person, her desires, her ability to take a trip had been challenged at numerous points because of racism. We can understand her anger as a perfectly acceptable response. But when hooks experienced murderous thoughts about her fellow passenger, she contends that her suppressed rage had become pathological.

At times, we repress our rage-response, but the denial of racism as a political and social problem that should make us angry creates a climate where rage becomes violent and self-defeating to the offended. hooks writes:

Racism can then be represented as an issue for blacks only, a mere figure of our perverse imaginations, while all whites continue to be brainwashed to deny the existence of an institutionalized racist structure that they work to perpetuate and maintain. (1995, p. 26)

In the same way that every response of outrage and rage at racism is dismissed as a fraudulent playing of the race card—thus intensifying the rage—tcontinual denial of the existence of institutionalized and culturally acceptable gender-based violence against black women creates situations where black women and girls either are denied the self-protective right to anger at violation or, worse, rage and outrage become the limits of black women's existence.

For hooks, Lorde, and Jordan, rage is the first movement toward community. Our anger tells us that we have a right to ourselves. When we recognize that others also have that right, for each of them to own themselves, we are able to create community with and for them. When we find ourselves angry with the communities to which we already belong because of where we live and how we are identified, as is the case with many urban black women who find themselves in danger in the public and private spaces of their neighborhoods and homes, we must make the move from rage to community transformation. But that is easier said than done.

As an interesting contrast, compare the girls in Miller's study and their reactions to Jordan's feelings of loneliness in the face of violence. Miller found that there was little to no intervention in school by administrators and teachers or by peers or adults in the neighborhood on behalf of harassed girls. While there was sometimes help to be found coming from brothers, male cousins, and friends, in the form of violent retaliation, more frequently, girls chose to defend themselves with rage. They noted that it was a matter of self respect that they should talk back to harassing boys. They did not did not value passive responses to male aggression and did not cower in the face of their torment (2008, p. 111). This desire to appear strong and defend themselves often resulted in more violent harassment. Miller calls this a "double bind":

Girls' responses to harassment, when assertive or aggressive, often resulted in more vicious mistreatment, especially in the forms of gender harassment and violent overtures. Their attempts to defend themselves were read by young men as disrespect, and the incidents quickly escalated into hostile confrontations when young women challenged young men's sexual and gender entitlements. Thus, young women were in a lose lose situation. Every available avenue for responding to sexual harassment reproduced their disempowered positions vis-à-vis young men. (Ibid., p. 99)

The girls in Miller's study sought self respect, even as they suffered further violence. Their individual efforts did not amount to an effective response to violence and harassment because they did not have a community that supported them.

What if the adults in the schools, in the community, in their homes had been outraged by the harassment? What if the people around the children learning to become abusers and harassers had chosen to come together as a community to solve the problem?

When we compare the stories told by the girls in Miller's study and Jordan's account of being raped, we see that Miller's findings support Jordan's contention that community is necessary for resistance. Jordan was able to generate rage and resist her white attacker because the existence of anti-racist community, even though no other person was present. While she did not prevent her physical violation, she was able to respond in a way that she found personally valuable and socially supported. In communities where offences against girls and women are commonplace and not seen as communal problems, the conditions of self-respect and safety, necessary for human flourishing and democracy, are greatly diminished.

According to Jordan, our struggles not merely to survive but to thrive are wrapped up in our feelings of belonging to a community. Like hooks and others, Jordan takes a position that attaches human flourishing with community but that also strongly prizes a concept of autonomy and self determination.

The two girls who were berated by the boys on the corner of 3rd and Main Streets in downtown, Dayton, Ohio, the day I began work on this chapter, may have done what Jody Miller writes that many of the girls in her study did, and what I have done many times in the face of assault—gotten angry and then attempted to write it off as an inevitable occurrence of everyday life. Such a concession, such a normalization of gender-based violation, is a survival tactic. In communities where women and girls have to choose survival because they find themselves the lone resisters to oppression, democracy has no chance. Fear cripples the resistance to oppression necessary for democracy and the formation of communities that would support individuals.

June Jordan illustrates this in an example in her "Notes toward a Model of Resistance." Recalling the lengths she and her students went to make sure that their protest of California's Proposition 209 would be lawful, she offers the story of a local attorney, whom they enlisted to help insure that the police called to break up their protest would understand that they were within their rights. Jordan writes:

> Rather than speak to the police, she started to tremble and cry. She said to me, "I can't. I can't do this. I'm just a single mother with three children." And so on. And it was awful to watch her fear making her powerless. It was awful. It was very depressing. And I thanked her for showing up, anyway. And I watched her retreat: Not blessed by a visible,

known, tested, and building community on which she could rely, she felt, and, therefore, she was isolated. She could not do herself, or anyone else, any good. (2002, p. 77)

Jordan connects the attorney's fear to the violation of rape. She writes that rape is the "dominator's determination to deprive you of your rights" (ibid., p. 77). When describing the rights that were being violated during the police attempts to break up the protest of Proposition 209, Jordan does not only list the constitutional right of peaceful assembly. She also includes, "needs for safe and self-respecting self determination" ibid., p. 76). The fearful attorney, like Jordan when she had been raped, could not resist because of feelings of isolation. Their isolation from communities of support limited their options for self-determination. Lack of belonging resulted in a decreased chance for autonomous action because of the fear domination engendered.

Jordan argued that "tapping into necessary, righteous rage" (ibid., p. 82), and, I would add, outrage, is the first step to begin to build communities of support. Until we get angry enough on our own behalves and that of others to resist oppression, our hopes for democratic community will fail. We all need to be upset that two black girls on the corner of 3rd and Main Streets in Dayton, Ohio, cannot walk to their bus without being harassed.

With hooks, Lorde, and Jordan, we must deny the pathology that tells us that our feelings of violation based on race and gender are not something we should make us angry. We should work to expose the forces of oppression and then work to change those forces. This work is work that requires us to recognize that without communities, individuals are more vulnerable to violation. Such an approach emphasizes the necessity of intentional community building. Without the support of others and public institutions, many urban black women and girls are destined live lives circumscribed by fear and violation. As Audre Lorde once said, "my fear of anger taught me nothing. Your fear of that anger will teach you nothing, also" (1984, p. 124).

Seven

A SKETCH OF THE MORAL RESPONSIBILITY TO ENGAGE OPPRESSORS

Courtland Lewis

1. Introduction

One of the most traumatic events that can happen to an individual is to be mentally or physically oppressed by some form of abuse or torture. Words are typically incapable of fully expressing the mental anguish that victims of such wrongdoings endure. Elaine Scarry illustrates, "Physical pain has no voice. . . . [it] does not simply resist language but actively destroys it" (1985, pp. 3–4). Nevertheless, *after* instances of oppression the destroyed voice returns; with this revitalization, individuals have an opportunity to engage the world anew, in positive ways.

One positive way of engaging the world is to foster a state of internal personal well-being and external social and political healing. I contend that victims, in the aftermath of oppression, have an obligation to engage the world in this way, by mentally or physically engaging their oppressors.

To show the reader why I hold such an intuition, I will examine two varying and important accounts of oppression, one offered by Miroslav Volf and the other by Adam Michnik. Volf's account illustrates his attempts to engage his interrogator/torturer (Captain G), several years after an ordeal, and centers on a series of imaginary meetings.

Some cases of oppression, such as spousal abuse and incest, cause such a high degree of mental and emotional damage that meeting with one's oppressor is not advised. Face-to-face meetings are not advised because of the power structure that exists between the individuals; a power structure that makes victims overly susceptible to their former oppressor. In such cases, victims can begin to blame themselves for the abuse they suffered, and find themselves entering back into the same oppressive relationships that existed before.

But such destructive possibilities are why Volf's account is so important: it provides an example of how victims can safely engage their oppressors without the dangers inherent in face-to-face meetings of this intimate sort. Volf shows readers how we should engage our oppressors and support the process of healing without actually physically engaging the person who has harmed us. Michnik's account, on the other hand, provides helpful insights into how physically engaging an oppressor face-to-face, when physical engagement is possible and advisable.

Volf and Michnik's respective accounts will serve as examples of the importance of engaging an oppressor, but to show that we have a moral obligation to engage our oppressors after cases of wrongdoing, I will introduce and briefly discuss two separate accounts of responsibility, respectively offered by Iris Marion Young and Slavenka Drakulić. These accounts will provide theoretical support for the obligation that I suggest exists.

The ability of any oppressed persons to engage their oppressors is limited by the extent to which they are oppressed, the events that take place after the wrongdoing, and other contextual circumstances that call for particular responses. Nevertheless, I maintain that an important moral dimension is part of engaging an oppressor. A careful examination of cases dealing with the aftermath of oppression and theories of shared responsibility illustrate a variety of reasons for believing such a moral obligation exists. In addition to the main thesis of this chapter regarding moral obligation to engage our oppressors, another of my goals is to foster a deeper understanding of what *ought* to happen post-war, post-atrocity, and post-oppression.

2. Accounts of Post-Oppression Engagement

Volf's book, *The End of Memory* (2006), revolves around his attempts to correctly remember the events that took place during his time as a prisoner and to search for a way of engaging and forgiving his former captor, Captain G. Volf's account of his struggles to deal with life after being falsely imprisoned and tortured is an intriguing and deeply spiritual account. It illustrates a case in which an individual desires and emotionally needs to engage his oppressor, but because of extraneous circumstances, cannot. Instead of giving up, however, he uses his imagination to achieve the engagement and healing that he desperately wants and needs.

Volf's account begins in Croatia in 1984, when he was called away from his American wife, his theological studies, and his dissertation criticizing Yugoslavia's communist government to serve a year in the Yugoslavian military. Unbeknownst to Volf, the government had been continually spying and keeping records on him and what they deemed his "subversive" activities. He was soon brought up on charges of being a spy, and, as a result, he was imprisoned, interrogated, and mentally and physically tortured. Volf survived his ordeal, and went on to become a talented author and theologian.

Due to circumstances beyond Volf's control, he is incapable of engaging his oppressor face-to-face, which is probably best for Volf because of the intimate type of oppression he endured. Unable to meet his oppressor, Volf decides to mentally engage Captain G by participating in a series of imaginary meetings designed to help him understand Captain G's motives and actions. These imaginative meetings take place in a public establishment, and are (at first) a complete failure: the conversation continually leads to accusations and denials from both Captain G and himself.

However, during their last meeting, Volf imagines the presence of a third party, Jesus Christ. With the imagined presence of Jesus at the conversation, Volf is able to have a brutally open and honest conversation with Captain G that allows himself to probe deep into his mental scars and to come to terms with Captain G's motives and actions. Volf uses his understanding of the teaching of Jesus (especially that of forgiveness) to move beyond the feelings of anger, revenge, and self-righteousness, to arrive at a point at which he is able to forgive Captain G. Volf feels as though he can move beyond the painful memories of his ordeal and he can cease to have his existence defined in relation to the wrongs committed against him. This healing and general state of well-being are the direct result of his mental engagement with his oppressor.

Whether an individual shares Volf's religious conviction, his imaginative exercise is important. Because of this sort of mental exercise, a victim is able to come to terms with the past, remember events correctly, and find that neither victim nor wrongdoer is defined only by the wrong that occurred. Volf, therefore, provides an example of engaging an oppressor within the general safety of an individual's mind, while promoting personal well-being.

One of my fears is that the obligation to engage oppressors after cases of oppression may be too much to require of victims. Fortunately, Volf shows that the engagement that I advocate comes in different forms and is amenable to different victims, wrongdoings, and circumstances.

The second example comes from Michnik. A complete examination of his social/political philosophy is beyond the scope of this chapter. However, several key components of Michnik's philosophy are key here, and he offers an exemplar for face-to-face engagement with oppressors in the aftermath of the oppression.

Michnik was a social dissident in communist Poland during the Cold War. He grew up in a household that was communist, free thinking, and well educated, and he was taught that the thoughtful criticism of views and positions was a virtue. Michnik grew up assuming that everyone would similarly value open-minded criticism. Therefore, he openly criticized many governmental personnel and policies, which he viewed as shortcomings in Poland's communist government. It never occurred to him that a government would interpret such critiques as a threat, especially since the critiques were only intended to foster the development of a more productive and fair communist society. Before long, he was shown the "error" of his thinking. With the loss of his naivety about the Poland's government and his realization that his criticisms were largely ineffective, he intensified his critiques and began participating with dissident groups such as Solidarity. A direct result of his intensified criticisms was that the government tracked of his activities, harassed and censored him when possible, and eventually jailed him for several years.

The hardships Michnik endured would be enough to make anyone bitter and full of hatred, but he responded quite differently. He used his time in jail to write and to develop a philosophy of political engagement based on *digni-ty*. Michnik's dignified engagement is founded on the requirement that we avoid the extremes of collaboration and ideological non-participantion (what he calls "maggots" and "angels"). Instead, we are obligated to respond to oppressors by continuing to engage them socially and politically while re-sisting the components of everyday life that might cause us to give up or act in an undignified or violent manner. Michnik opines that we can never for-get that we exist in a complex world of overlapping concerns, motivations, and forces that influence how individuals act and responds to external socio-political forces.

Michnik does not merely philosophize about how to act; instead, he ac-tively practices the type of engagement that he views as necessary for a healthy soul and healthy society. The best example of this sort of engagement is seen in a conversation he had with Woljciech Jaruzelski, the communist leader of Poland who oppressed dissention by enacting a strict policy of mar-tial law. In this conversation, Michnik notes how his perception of his op-pressor (Jaruzelski) evolved from viewing him as some despicable bureaucrat to viewing him as a normal person. Referring to his first meeting with Jaru-zelski, Michnik writes:

> There was no sign of the wickedness that I'd imagined for years. Later, I became convinced that it's impossible to gain a correct impression of what kind of person General Jaruzelski is just by reading his speeches. (1998, 261)

What Michnik says holds true for almost everyone. Too often, we create images of those who harm us, unrealistic images of their inhumanness. But Michnik illustrates how these preconceived notions are often wrong, because we forget about the existential pressures that exist within our social and polit-ical world.

Michnik's conversation with Jaruzelski shows that an actual engage-ment with an oppressor is not only possible but mutually beneficial; it is also beneficial to society writ large. Not only does Michnik's conversation begin the healing process for him and for his oppressor, but it also promotes healing in Poland and around the world. His conversation is an example of the digni-fied engagement for which he argues—engagement with, but opposition against, to foster a healthy society. He poignantly writes:

> The maturity of nations, societies, and individuals is measured in terms of the way in which they live with their own history and their own life story. . . . I think it of great significance—and in some ways I count it a victory for both of us—that today we are able to talk about all this [the oppression and dissention] without hatred, without hostility, and with mutual respect while remaining true to our own pas. (Ibid., p. 285)

This type of dignified engagement is the hallmark of the philosophy of Dr. Martin Luther King, Jr. and Mahatma Gandhi, and is one of the most valuable results of engaging one's oppressor face-to-face.

The cases presented by Volf and Michnik illustrate two types of engagement that I propose are required of individuals after cases of oppression. Not everyone will be capable of directly engaging one's oppressor as Michnik does, but anyone can engage them imaginatively, or through some spiritual or psychological experience as Volf did. Imaginative engagement might even foster the ability to have the face-to-face engagement that Michnik is capable of, which then might have the added result of promoting a state of reconciliation or forgiveness. The next thing to do is to tie these two accounts into a consistent notion of shared responsibility.

3. Three Notions of Responsibility

The respective accounts offered by Volf and Michnik evince powerful examples of oppressed individuals who engaged their oppressors in unique ways. Even if we accept these accounts as paradigm cases of what should happen after instances of oppression, however, still nothing has been said about the existence of a general moral obligation or responsibility to engage oppressors, post-oppression.

This section suggests that such a moral responsibility does exist by examining two accounts of shared responsibility. (I will use obligation and responsibility interchangeably to refer to the moral state of affairs when one is morally required to act in a specific way under specific circumstances; for example, "One ought to do X, if Y occurs.")

The first understanding of responsibility comes from Iris Marion Young, who argues for a social connection model of responsibility based on the social processes in which we are all engaged. Young states, "Obligations of justice arise between persons by virtue of the social processes that connect them; political institutions are the response to these obligations rather than their basis" (2006, p. 102). Young is concerned with harms that can result from decisions made from within the structure of society. She discusses decisions we make locally that may have global moral repercussions. According to Young, "The fact that some structural social processes connect people across the world without regard to political boundaries" (ibid., p. 102) creates moral responsibilities to those affected by our actions and decisions. Consequently, we all have obligations to those whom we directly or indirectly harm, and we are responsible, to varying degrees, for discharging these responsibilities. Young says, "All agents who contribute by their actions to the structural processes that produce injustice have responsibilities to work to remedy these injustices" (ibid., pp. 102–103).

Young suggests that we all have a level of shared responsibility via the social connections within a community, society in general, and the political system in which we participates. Such an account is important for my purpose because it implies that victims have responsibilities that lie outside of themselves, and that individual members of society have obligations to victims.

After cases of oppression, victims must not forget that they exist within a set of social connections that produce responsibilities. The responsibilities of such individuals will undoubtedly be severely limited as a result of their oppression, but they exist nonetheless. One such responsibility is that victims are obligated to promote their mental well-being by coming to terms with the oppression they have endured. This does not mean that victims do not retain the right to be angry and to grieve, but at some point, they must strive to move beyond (and cease to be defined by) their oppression if they are to be physically, mentally, and morally healthy.

This shared responsibility is also the foundation for a second responsibility: victims have a responsibility to promote the well-being of society. Since individuals comprise society, each individual's well-being is significant to society's well-being as a whole. Therefore, engaging oppressors, and fostering individual well-being, helps bring about the well-being of society. It promotes a society that has confronted and learned to address and avoid the conditions that allow for oppression.

Jessica Wolfendale provides an argument that illustrates the importance of Young's social connection model. She argues that to view wrongdoers as *not* worthy of any sort of engagement is to adopt aspects of the wrongdoer's moral outlook, and doing so makes us more prone to commit the same types of wrongdoing when given the chance (2005). If Wolfendale is correct, then by not accepting our responsibility to engage our oppressors, we not only limit our (and society's) ability to heal from an act of oppression, but we also take on the same mentality of our oppressors, which only leads to more oppression.

On the other hand, individuals that comprise society have their own sets of responsibilities that must be discharged. They must recognize and acknowledge their responsibility for allowing oppression to occur within their society. They must assume the responsibility to promote societal conditions that do not allow for oppression, and they must promote conditions where engagement between victims and wrongdoers can safely occur. If we are to a achieve a healthy society after cases of oppression, and help victims of oppression, then the individual members of that society must be involved in process of healing too.

The next understanding of responsibility comes from Slavenka Drakulić. Drakulić's understanding of responsibility arose from her first visit to Tel Aviv and Croatia's (her home country) political responses to the memory of the Holocaust. During her visit to Tel Aviv, Drakulić was continually questioned about her responsibility—as a Croatian—for the Holocaust.

During World War II, Croatia was guilty of exterminating approximately 17,000 Jews, Serbs, gypsies, and Croat communists, but these events occurred before she was even born (1996, pp. 136–137). Drakulić was surprised when she was asked by several different people whether she felt any regret or guilt for what the Croats did during the war. Her response was something along the lines of, sure, I hate that such events occurred, but I had nothing to do with them.

The more time she spent in Tel Aviv around those who actually suffered in concentration camps, the more she came to realize that her response was unsatisfactory. After careful consideration, she realized:

> in front of the victims and their relatives, it was much easier to defend yourself from the past than from the present. As far as the past was concerned, I could offer my regrets, but it was much more difficult to explain what the Croatian government and Croatian citizens were doing today to deal with that past. (Ibid., p. 139)

> Every Croatian citizen bears a responsibility for his silent support of this government's attitude toward the Holocaust," which at the time was comprised of fascists who honored their fascist ancestors by naming streets after those who participated in the Holocaust. (Ibid., p. 140)

According to Drakulić, her connection to Croatia and Croatia's history was defining her. She suggests the entities with which we identify (in this case, country) creates a level of responsibility for the past actions of that entity. She claims that the past is everyone's problem. We must take responsibility for the historical attitudes of the groups with which we identify that led to oppression, because we are responsible for the current attitudes of those entities with which we identify. Drakulić concludes:

> When directly faced with the question of personal responsibility, a person cannot view history as a series of incomprehensible acts of a leader or a government. Eventually he must understand that it also depends upon what he himself says and does. In post-communist Croatia, we don't have a good excuse for our silence any more. (Ibid., p. 142)

Drakulić's account of responsibility shows that we must be careful about which ideas and entities with which we identify. Like Young, she suggests that we are obligated to actively work toward ensuring the entities with which we identify (country, state, social group, religion) do not promote destructive ideas. If we do not discharge this responsibility, then we are passively promoting the wrongs committed under the auspices of those ideas. Drakulić holds that we are responsible for the thoughts with which we identify, so we must not identify with destructive thoughts, one being vengeance.

Volf and Michnik serve as exemplars of Young and Drakulic's notions of shared responsibility because they promote identifying with a set of positive moral stances that promotes the health and well-being of the individual and society.

I maintain that these two understandings of responsibility, combined with the true examples of Volf and Michnik, suggest that a moral responsibility exists to engage oppressors after cases of oppression. Each understanding shows how we are responsible for intrapersonal features of our life and interpersonal features of others' lives, who comprise society at large.

4. Confronting a Significant Criticism

Let us confront one significant criticism that may be waged against the moral responsibility suggested in this essay. It suggests victims of oppression are powerless, and that powerless individuals have no power to engage oppressors. If anyone has a moral responsibility, it contends, the oppressor has the responsibility to seek forgiveness or reconciliation with the victim. As Martian Luther King, Jr. suggests, imagining a powerless individual as having power is difficult; responsibility to engage or seek reconciliation with one's oppressor might be thought to be even more difficult. However, I contend, although individuals might feel powerless in the face of oppressors or under the press of a corrupt governmental system, the individual *always* maintains some facet of power over socio-political forces.

Václav Havel explains the phenomenon of the "power of the powerless." He claims "existential pressures" and "existential vulnerabilities" affect us all, and that these pressures and vulnerabilities explain the dynamic relationship between individuals and socio-political forces. Such existential occurrences become acute when individuals begin losing their individuality and attempt to exist in a system that keeps them in a constant state of fear.

Havel gives us the example of a storeowner who places a sign that reads "Workers of the world unite!" in his storefront window because of his fear of being oppressed by the people and his government (1992, p. 54). The storeowner feels pressure from those in power, but instead of resisting, he helps bolster their power to oppress by showing support for their socio-political agenda. The storeowner, therefore, legitimizes the state by promoting their agenda. According to Havel, the storeowner should resist the government's agenda by not displaying the sign. We are all to resist oppressive regimes in whatever way possible, no matter how big or small, and it is this resistance that culminates in the power of the powerless. Our gestures of acceptance or rejection of ideas and actions reverberate throughout society as a sign to other individuals and the government in power, and they either lend power to or set up competing power structures to them both.

The indirect or passive acceptance and fear of the system keeps governmental and oppressive systems in power. When we abdicate our power, and blindly follow the "higher authority" of a corrupt society or government, we become collaborators with them. As Havel claims, if we fail to resist, and therefore promote oppressive socio-political forces, we "confirm the system, fulfill the system, make the system, [are] the system" (Havel, 1992, p. 136).

The same conclusion holds for all individuals who relinquish their individuality for the security of life under the control of a corrupt, undignified system. The system cannot survive if individuals maintain their individuality and resist it. Havel claims that the powerlessness of the individual who struggles to maintain one's individuality creates "parallel structures" that rival the system in place. The individual's fight for dignity, therefore, gives both the individual and society power: what Havel calls the "power of the powerless" (ibid., p. 192).

5. Concluding Remarks

With the accounts of Volf and Michnik, and the two understandings of responsibility offered by Young and Drakulic, we can draw several significant conclusions concerning the moral responsibility of victims of oppression in the aftermath of oppression. These conclusions must remain incomplete until a more in-depth and detailed analysis can be performed, but I will offer three of them here to spur further analysis.

First, we should not give up on those who harm us. I will not offer a defense of individuals who actively oppress others, but as Socrates suggests, we act only in accordance with what we think is good. Individuals do not lose their worth as human beings just because they harm someone. As Volf and Michnik show, their respective captors have "good" (although they disagree with them) reasons for why they did what they did. Victims do not have to agree with the reasons a wrongdoer offers, but understanding those reasons helps them reconcile themselves to the harm that occurred. By engaging our oppressors, we reject the ideas that foster oppression, and we not only change ourselves, but we foster positive change in both the oppressor and society at large.

Second, crucial to individuals' well-being is that they engage their oppressors. The obligation suggested in this essay is not supposed to be an overbearing responsibility that forces victims to do something against their will. Otherwise, the obligation itself would be oppressive. Instead, it is designed to promote healing in victims, wrongdoers, and society.

Third, that we engage our oppressors is crucial to the social structure in which we all live and participate. By engaging oppressors, we are promoting a new set of ideas that is antithetical to oppression. By engaging oppressors, we foster positive social and political change while denouncing oppression; this is healthy for everyone.

If the consequences of these three conclusions were sufficient to show that there exists a moral responsibility to one's oppressor, then the project sketched in the essay would be complete. However, merely pointing out several good consequences that an action brings about is not enough to show that the action should be considered a universal moral responsibility. Therefore, much more work needs to be done; work for which the sketch offered in this essay will hopefully serve as a catalyst.

Eight

THE RADICAL PRAXIS OF TEACHING FOR A JUST COMMUNITY: MARCUSE AND KRISTEVA ON LIBERATING THE SUBJECT

Tanya Loughead

1. Introduction

This chapter locates itself within the bold proclamation of Herbert Marcuse in his book, *The Aesthetic Dimension: Toward a Critique of Marxist Aesthetics* (1978). In this, his final book, Marcuse criticizes Marxism (and most Marxists) for taking a too narrow approach to revolution and not seeing the ways in which civilization moves or progresses—thus, not able to grasp the various ways of revolution that would make sense and promote liberation and the just community of a "new world order." Marxists, he claims, have largely ignored the individual and the emotional life of the individual, thus ignoring a large possible site of revolution. This is perhaps their greatest fault and blind-spot in desiring revolution. He writes:

> The subjectivity of individuals, their own consciousness and unconscious tends to be dissolved into class conscious. Thereby, a major prerequisite of revolution is minimized, namely the fact that the need for radical change must be rooted in individuals themselves, in their intelligence and their passions, their drives and their goals (ibid., pp. 3–4).

When we seek a just community, we must at the same time discuss individuals and their oppressors. From this foundation based on Marcuse's ideas, I move to the argument of Julia Kristeva in "Psychoanalysis and Freedom," from her book *Intimate Revolt: The Powers and Limits of Psychoanalysis* (2002). Therein, she describes the process of analysis as an act of liberating the individual. But, as we will see, this liberation is not freedom from the community, but freedom to engage.

This chapter follows the path of Kristeva's argument, all the while dissecting the process, not of analysis, but of radical teaching. Overall, it defends two positions, the first inspired by Kristeva and the second by Marcuse: (1) that radical teaching is an act of freeing the individual; and (2) that just communities can be sought by liberated individuals, who are in a continual state of revolution/revolutionizing.

2. Marcuse

My chapter begins from the end, basing the majority of my argument founda-
tionally and primarily upon the last work that Marcuse wrote, *The Aesthetic
Dimension*. I will add only a few references from Marcuse's work on Sigmund Freud, *Eros and Civilization* (1966), that will lead us to Kristeva's
comments on revolution and psychoanalysis.

   The Aesthetic Dimension is a fascinating (and to my mind, damning and
accurate) description of the kinds of liberation we now need and how they
might arise. Marcuse's main point, with which I heartily agree, is that revolution has been framed only in terms of large-scale social movements—
typically in or against government. The French Revolution is held up as the
epitome of this kind of revolution: an entire people rise up together to fight a
system that takes no account of their interests. I argue, with Marcuse, that this is
a far too narrow definition of revolution. It is not the kind of revolution that is
likely to bring about the kinds of changes that we need in our current society.

   Marcuse clearly and absolutely links art with revolution. Marxists, he
claims, have largely ignored the individual and the emotional life of the individual, thus ignoring a large possible site of revolution. This is perhaps Marxism's greatest fault and blind-spot in desiring revolution: "It is all too easy to
relegate love and hate, joy and sorrow, hope and despair, to the domain of
psychology, thereby removing them from the concerns of radical praxis"
(Marcuse, 1978, p. 5). In this line of criticism, he writes:

> The subjectivity of individuals, their own consciousness and uncons-
> cious tends to be dissolved into class conscious. Thereby, a major prere-
> quisite of revolution is minimized, namely the fact that the need for rad-
> ical change must be rooted in individuals themselves, in their intelli-
> gence and their passions, their drives and their goals. (Ibid., pp. 3–4)

In Marxism, he writes, "subjectivity became an atom of objectivity"; whereas
what Marcuse hopes for is the "rebirth of the rebellious subjectivity" (ibid.,
pp. 4, 7). Art is invaluable in this rebirth. The work of art, "re-presents reality
while accusing it," and "stands under the law of the given while transgressing
this law" and has the "power to break the monopoly of established reality"
(ibid., pp. 8, 11, 9).

   Charles Reitz, in his book *Art, Alienation and the Humanities,* claims
that in *The Aesthetic Dimension*:

> there is a turn in Marcuse's theorizing, almost a reversal," away from
> the "militant activist positions" of his earlier works "to an explicit reas-
> sertion of certain of the most contemplative values and assumptions of
> classical European aesthetics" (2000, p. 195).

I agree with Reitz that there is a marked shift in Marcuse's work by the time of his writing *The Aesthetic Dimension*, but I disagree that Marcuse loses or departs from any of his "militant activist positions." Those activist positions have now found hope for revolution from within the aesthetic experience, as an additional and crucial site of revolution. This is the revolution of individuals, their "passions, drives and goals," as quoted above. Revolution cannot take place at the level of class alone, Marcuse realizes by the time he writes his final work. He explains:

> Art can preserve its truth, it can make conscious the necessity of change, only when it obeys its own law against that of reality. . . . Art cannot change the world, but it can contribute to changing the consciousness and drives of the men and women who could change the world. (1978, p. 32)

Marxist aesthetics, unfortunately, devalues "the entire realm of subjectivity" (ibid., p. 3). This is "reductionistic" and "brackets the particular content of individual consciousness and, with it, the subjective potential for revolution" (ibid., p. 4).

Whether Marcuse believes that only art can provoke this subjective revolutionary potential remains unclear to me. Because my thesis indicates that I want to take Marcuse's ideas in a slightly different direction, I acknowledge that, in many places in the text, Marcuse does appear to be arguing that *only art* can bring the kind of shift he seeks. In this sense, at several places in the text, Marcuse's argument may oppose my project. Such examples include:

> The thesis of the book is that "the radical qualities of art, that is to say, its indictment of the established reality and its invocation of the beautiful image of liberation are grounded precisely where art *transcends* its social determination and emancipates itself." (Ibid., p. 6)

Later he says, "And in the intellectual culture of our society, it is the aesthetic form which, by virtue of its otherness, can stand up against this integration" (ibid., p. 50), and, "The revolution is for the sake of life not death. Here is the perhaps most profound kinship between art and revolution" (ibid., p. 56). Most clearly, "Art breaks open a dimension inaccessible to other experience, a dimension in which human beings, nature, and things no longer stand under the law of the established reality" (ibid., p. 72). Or more simply, "the truth of art lies in its power to break the monopoly of established reality" (ibid., p. 9).

On the other hand, I want to keep Marcuse's overall critique that Marxist theory has been blind to the plural modes of revolution. I would say not only Marxist notions, but popular notions of what a revolution is have been constituted by this narrowness. Therefore, I end this section by listing some of Marcuse's text that supports my thesis. Marcuse claims we need to shift "the locus of the individual's realization from the domain of the performance principle and the profit motive to that of the inner resources of the human being: passion, imagination, conscience" (ibid., p. 5). This is not mere inwardness and withdrawal from society; this shift in conscience must strive to "break out" into "the material and intellectual culture" (ibid.). Most importantly, throughout the text, Marcuse emphasizes our paying attention to the drives, desires and emotions of individuals, to which the earlier passages I have cited attest.

3. Hart on the Phenomenological Reduction

In widening what we mean by revolution, alongside Marcuse, I reap ideas from James G. Hart's theory of the university and the humanities as astutely spelled out in his article, "The Essential Look (*eidos*) of the Humanities" (2008). Therein, Hart does a masterful job of applying the Husserlian notion of the *epoché* (bracketing) to modes of learning in the university. He offers a harsh criticism of the modern American university, which, he says, is today, hardly more than "a contingent assortment of unrelated and capricious departments housed in a kind of department store for consumers looking for job training" (ibid., p. 110). He chides those "departments in the store" of the university for being seen as successful to the degree that they "advance the growth interests of the corporations, the degree to which the university is able to serve the nationalist or imperialist impulses of the state."

Hart observes that, under this system, "the nature of the university becomes increasingly occluded by and subordinated to capitalist economics and nation-statism" (ibid., p. 111). Further: "money transfer, capital and investment possibilities" are the center of the university's concerns and what "carries most weight" are "student recruitment, administration politics, the athletic department, the university offices for economic development, ROTC, the School of Business, the amount of corporate and government grants given to the faculty, the size of the super computer, [and] the number of superstars residing in and orbiting around the particular university" (ibid., pp. 110–111). In the university defined thusly, "the humanities become the whimsical wispy decoration for the real work of the university" (ibid.).

So, what is to be done, what is the way out? Where is the revolutionary potential in our universities (again, other than in the obvious places like encouraging students to protest and the like)?

Hart argues that, within the broad spectrum of programs and departments within the university, *the humanities can serve as the phenomenological reduction*. He writes, "Much of the modern university, and surely the ancient one too, functions in what phenomenology calls the 'natural attitude.' This attitude is how we are for the most part in the world" (ibid., p. 113). The phenomenological reduction is the bracketing of the natural attitude that we usually take with regards to the world around us—the things we assume, the attitudes and stances that we take for granted.

The *epoché* tries to bring us to a neutral stance, neither affirming nor denying the "facts" of the world and myself. It is in this way that consciousness and the world can be explored with less bias or predisposition. It does not ask about the objects of perception, but backs up to ask, what is perception, how do we arrive at it? Hart admits that if biologists are "finding out the DNA structure of a species of soybean" then for them, it might be an "unnatural and distracting intrusion" to reflect upon the act of perception itself (ibid., p. 114).

So, Hart is not suggesting that the reduction *replace* all other forms of research. The problem is that "to the extent that the scientistic or naturalistic attitude gains a hegemony in all facets of our life," at that point, "the natural sciences appear as the only true forms of knowing and all the other disciplines must take their bearings from these" (ibid., p. 115). "The natural attitude is normative here as well in almost all of our life," whereas "reflection on the *bringing to light* rather than on *what* is brought to light" (ibid., p. 114) is the task of those of us in the humanities.

Hart's critique of the modern university assists me in spelling out what I would like to do with late Marcuse: use his ideas on the revolution of the individual (through art), and apply them to the manner in which universities can and should teach as sites of radical critique, in the original meaning of that term, turning to the root of how, what, and why we study at all.

Next, I turn to Kristeva who helps me to further explain revolution through the freedom of the individual as a re-birth.

4. Kristeva

Readers may wonder why I chose to use a text of Kristeva's on psychoanalysis to talk about freedom and teaching when plenty of literature on radical teaching exists, such as that of Paulo Freire and his many followers, and because Kristeva, in the first line of the article upon which I will rely heavily, admits, "freedom is not a psychoanalytic concept" (2002, p. 225). In reply I say, despite her beginnings, by the end of the article, freedom is where Kristeva has arrived.

According to Kristeva, freedom is the ultimate goal in psychoanalysis, although of course, at the same time, hardly any philosopher in the past fifty years (within the Continental tradition) believes in the complete freedom and autonomy of the subject. Postmodern theory has itself (in league with psychoanalysis) been charged with being utterly apolitical and relativistic (a charge mostly seen in the United States). Here I am thinking of, for instance the vitriolic attacks on Jacques Derrida—in place of obituaries—that ran in papers such as the *New York Times* the day after his death.

In a more academic vein, Fredric Jameson accuses postmodernism of being about superficiality, commodification, ahistoricism, and "essential triviality"—although, granted, Jameson makes these charges to expect more from postmodern times (1991, p. 46). He writes that within the postmodern milieu, it will be nearly impossible:

> for political groups . . . to intervene in history and to modify its otherwise passive momentum," since this postmodern mode of being transforms the past "into visual mirages, stereotypes or texts, effectively abolish[ing] any practical sense of future and of the collective project. (Ibid.)

For a lucid explanation of the issues at hand, read Douglas Kellner and Steven Best's works, for instance "Postmodern Theory: Critical Interrogations" (1997) or, "Postmodern Politics and the Battle for the Future," where they write, "as with postmodern theory, there is no one 'postmodern politics,' but rather a conflicting set of positions that emerges from the ambiguities of social change and multiple postmodern theoretical perspectives" (2002).

While thoroughly refuting the claim that postmodern theory is apolitical is beyond the scope of this chapter, evidence for it exists. For instance, one reading of Foucault's work could lead us to the impression that the subject has no power, no possibility for an authentic or self-directed subjectivity outside of the power structures that shape and define us. Evidence can also be found against it. For instance, in Derrida's work, readers find a profound and endless ethical and political duty placed on the subject. John Caputo writes in his obituary of Derrida:

> Deconstruction, it turns out, is not nihilism; it just has high standards! Deconstruction is satisfied with nothing because it is waiting for the Messiah, which Derrida translated into the philosophical figure of the "to come" (*à venir*), the very figure of the future (*l'avenir*), of hope and expectation. Deconstruction's meditation on the contingency of our beliefs and practices—on democracy, for example—is made in the name of a promise that is astir in them, for example, of a democracy "to come" for which every existing democracy is but a faint predecessor state. (2004, p. 8)

I side with Derrida and his readers, Caputo and Judith Butler, among many others, who—although we would all admit that no central "I" exists outside of the structures, systems, and symbolic order that form us and our desires—believe nonetheless that there is room for the profound and deep responsibility and the possible freedom of the individual. As I understand it, freedom is not a given, but a task or a *goal*. No "core" of freedom lies beneath the layers of our oppressions (as if it lies there waiting to be unburied); freedom must be *built*. Autonomy does not exist first, and is then stripped away. Autonomy—never total—is a goal.

Kristeva's article follows the trajectory of freedom in psychoanalytic thought. She begins with Freud, who assigns freedom "the meaning of an instinctual impulse shackled by the human need to live in a community" (2002, p. 225). For him, freedom stands up against, and is antagonistic to, civilization. To quote Freud from *Civilization and Its Discontents*, "the liberty of the individual is no gift of civilization" and "the urge for freedom, therefore, is directed against particular forms and demands of civilization or against civilization altogether" (1961, pp. 49, 50).

Kristeva writes that, for Freud, "moral consciousness and its organ the superego, thus impose from mankind's beginning a renouncement of the instinctual freedoms" (2002, p. 226). Yet, at the same time, Freud warns us against a kind of nostalgia that, while "it seems certain that we do not feel comfortable in our present-day civilization, . . . it is very difficult to form an opinion whether and in what degree men of an earlier age felt happier" (1961, p. 41). Freud writes:

> When we start considering this possibility, we come upon a contention which is so astounding what we must dwell on it. This contention holds that what we call our civilization is largely responsible for our misery, and that we should be much happier if we gave it up and returned to primitive conditions. (1961, p. 38)

Freud's understanding of freedom is a "naturalist," "I can" understanding of caprice and drive without restriction—yet that does not imply that freedom is a higher or better state than that in which man exists in civilized life. This drive becomes desire through understanding that a mature human can only think of desires and freedom through communally shared language that "checks impulse and command" (Kristeva, 2002, p. 228).

Kristeva follows the path from Freud to Jacques Lacan. Yet, to my mind, Kristeva's reading of Lacan is more innovative than she gives herself credit for. She claims that Lacan maintains "subjective interiority" "radicalized to the extreme" (Kristeva, 2002, p. 230). Through the process of analysis, the subject is now authorized to "discover his desire and to explore his own limits" (ibid.). Though, of course, this authorization is always already structured by language, forces, expectations, norms, hierarchies—in short, by the symbolic order in which subjects must find their "place." I always read Lacan as leaving very little latitude for subjects to do any of their own "discovery of desire," that "own" being a construction anyway since the subject is always already in the grips of the non-subjective.

In Freud's terminology, the subject can never escape civilization and thus, can never really be "free" in the pure "naturalist" sense that Kristeva first describes. The new freedom, freedom as desire and not drive, is what Kristeva explores and finds fertile.

Psychoanalysis is "anti-normativist." Both Kristeva and Paul Ricouer (1970) write that in the behaviorist United States, the overall goal of engaging in therapy is to get the patient in-line with the "norms" of society. This creates several problems for feminists and those who fight for justice.

Why "normatize" people to an unjust world? A therapist is then a collaborationist with injustice, by "healing/aligning" a patient to the systems and ideals of an unjust society. (One need only think of being a woman in so-called marriage therapy during the mid-twentieth century to imagine this kind of hell.) I am in complete agreement with Kristeva when she writes that psychoanalysis is "not only anti-normativist" but also "in implicit polemic with ego psychology," which points to the "discomfort" that psychoanalysis always encounters and "will always encounter" in "the moralizing universe of technology and adaptation" (2002, p. 230).

I argue a parallel can be drawn between behaviorist therapy and the kind of "normativist" teaching that would be a collusion with what Hart called the "natural attitude" of the world and university—an education that replicates the corporate model of beliefs, similar to what Freire called the "banking" concept of education (2000, Chapter 2)—education as an accumulation of facts that *matter to* and *prepare us for* the present state of (unquestioned) affairs and values. To keep with Kristeva's language, this is what we might call a normativist education, as opposed to what, with Freire, I am advocating, is an anti-normativist education, just as psychoanalysis is an anti-normative therapy. I am sketching a kind of *momentary polemic* for the purposes of just the kind of *dichotomy* that Kristeva suggests:

Behaviorist therapy   ◄────────►   Psychoanalysis
Current state of the university ◄────────►   Humanities
Normative   ◄────────►   Radical

5. Conclusion

Returning to Hart, we recall that he claimed that most of what was going on in the contemporary university was normative—that the natural attitude is normative, and that the humanities have the most radical potential due to the *epoché* that they can provoke. According to Kristeva, Lacan's ideal in therapy is neither to bend patients to the society that surrounds them, nor to let subjects have free reign on their desires. Here is a passage where Kristeva describes the kind of freedom that is possible in Lacanian psychoanalysis:

> For if the analyst's benevolent neutrality allows the patient not to yield to his desire, it is not less true that we greet this freedom with a certain number of ideals. . . . His listening and interpretation welcome these desires based on a moral choice that constitutes an ethic: it is not instructive but it is not without communal objectives. . . . Lacan himself evokes a few of his ideals: to make the patient capable of love, to favor authenticity against "as if" personalities or "false selves," to reinforce independence. (2002, p. 231)

If psychoanalysis is successful, it puts the subject into a constant state of rebirth. This is a rebirth of the subject not internally so that an individual could be free *from* others, but freedom to internalize the outside and to engage *with* others. Here Kristeva's originality shines. She describes a mature subject free from acting defensively toward the outside world, toward the community. The perpetual rebirth that she describes is rebirth to openness. Her hopes for psychoanalysis are high—she writes:

> Let us say without false modesty: no modern experience aside from psychoanalysis offers man the chance to restart his psychical life, and thus, quite simply, life itself, opening up choices that guarantee the *plurality of an individual's capacity for connection.* (Ibid.)

She continues, "This version of freedom is perhaps the most precious and most serious gift that psychoanalysis has given mankind" (2002, p. 234, emphasis added). For Kristeva, psychoanalysis is one part of "civilization" that, contra Freud, rather than decreasing individuals' freedom, increases their freedom by fostering their ability to make connections and links. It is by understanding ourselves, our history, and *how* we have othered others in our lives that, from that understanding, we are able to re-birth ourselves into new relations, new others, new eyes.

This re-birthing of the self is precisely what Kristeva denotes when she reminds us that the original meaning of revolution—re-volt—is to cause a re-birthing, a new start, a turning around. In another work of hers, *The Sense and Non-Sense of Revolt* (2000), she turns our attention to the etymology through the Latin words "*volvere*" (the womb, esp. of a sow) and "*volte*" (times) and links them to derivative terms "curve," "curvature," and "turn/return," but also movement in time such as "turning back," or "wrapping" among others. This re-volting of subjects allows, "[to] attenuate his sufferings, to relocate his desires, and to restart his creativity—indefinitely" (Kristeva, 2002, p. 238). One of the last points that she makes in her essay is, "the aptitude for this revolt leads the analyzed person to re-create links, suggesting that the analytical experience is at the source of a serious humanism" (ibid., p. 237).

I suggested earlier that freedom is not a given, but a *goal*; that autonomy is not at our core, but to be *built*. With Kristeva, I believe that this autonomy is never built apart from others and in opposition to them, but in concert with them and with their assistance. Others help me (and I can choose to help them) remove their blocks toward openness per se.

M. Jacqui Alexander, in her book, *Pedagogies of Crossing*, compares the economy and the academy. One manner of comparison is that "universities provide workers for the economy" (2005, p. 106). She writes that the "ideological attack" against multiculturalism and feminism makes a statement about:

the kind of worker that the transnational empire requires—a worker who fits into an already assigned place within the productive process, without a critical examination of how she got there and who is there with her. (Alexander, 2005, pp. 106–107)

Bad teaching and bad therapy have a similar—though usually unspoken—goal, and Alexander describes it as well as anyone: a human being who "fits into an already assigned place," be that a worker on the assembly line, a student in med school, a "good wife," or "a breadwinner for the family."

What I am suggesting has similarities to Martin Heidegger's sense of *das Nicht-zuhause-sein*—that which constantly reminds us that we are not at home, that authenticity requires we always question our home, our "assignment," our place in the world. Radical education undoes the assignment of place. It un-assigns and rebirths, not just once, but sets up that re-volting to reoccur throughout our lives.

WORKS CITED

Chapter One
William C. Gay

Cady, Duane. (1991) "War, Gender, Race & Class," *Concerned Philosophers For Peace Newsletter*, 11:2 (Fall), pp. 4–10.

Comstock, Gary David. (1991). *Violence Against Lesbians and Gay Men*. New York: Columbia University Press.

Darwin, Charles. (1962) *The Origin of Species*. New York: Collier Books.

Engel, J. Ronald. (1993) "The Role of Ethics, Culture, and Religion in Conserving Biodiversity: A Blueprint for Research and Action." In *Ethics, Religion, and Biodiversity: Relations between Conservation and Cultural Values*. Edited by Lawrence S. Hamilton. Cambridge, UK: The While Horse Press.

Fukuyama, Francis. (1992) *The End of History and the Last Man*. New York: Free Press.

Gallie, W. B. (1978) *Philosophers of Peace and War: Kant, Clausewitz, Marx, Engels, and Tolstoy*. Cambridge, UK: Cambridge University Press.

Galtung, Johan. (1982) *Environment, Development, and Military Activity*. New York: Columbia University Press.

Gay, William C. (1976) "Action versus Society: The Significance of Weber and Marx in the Intellectual History of the Social Disciplines," *Cultural Hermeneutics*, 4:1 (November), pp. 1–23.

———. (1985) "Nuclear War: Public and Governmental Misconceptions," pp. 11–25. In *Nuclear War: Philosophical Perspectives*. Edited by Michael Allen Fox and Leo Groarke. New York: Peter Lang Publishing.

———. (1987) "Nuclear Discourse and Linguistic Alienation," *Journal of Social Philosophy*, 18:2 (Summer), pp. 42–49.

———. (1989) "From Nuclear Winter to Hiroshima: Nuclear Weapons and the Environment." In *Issues in War and Peace: Philosophical Inquiries*, pp. 189–205. Edited by Joseph Kunkel and Kenneth Klein. Wolfeboro, N.H.: Longwood Academic.

———. (1990) "The Russell-Hook Debates of 1958: Arguments from the Extremes on Nuclear War and the Soviet Union," pp. 79–95. In *In the Interest of Peace: A Spectrum of Philosophical Perspectives*. Edited by Kenneth H. Klein and Joseph C. Kunkel. Wakefield, N.H.: Longwood Academic.

———. (1994) "The Prospect for a Nonviolent Model of National Security," pp. 119–134. In *On the Eve of the 21st Century: Perspectives of Russian and American Philosophers*. Edited by William Gay and T. A. Alekseeva. Lanham, Md.: Rowman and Littlefield.

———. (1996) "Environmental Issues, Pollution, and The Military," pp. 132–135. In *An Encyclopedia of War and Ethics*. Edited by Donald A. Wells. Westport, Conn.: Greenwood Publishers.

———. (1998a) "Exposing and Overcoming Linguistic Alienation and Linguistic Violence," *Philosophy and Social Criticism*, 24:2/3, pp. 137–156.

———. (1998b) "The Practice of Linguistic Nonviolence," *Peace Review*. 10:4, pp. 545–547.

———. (1999) "Linguistic Violence," pp. 13–34. In *Institutional Violence*. Edited by Deane Curtin and Robert Litke. Amsterdam: Rodopi.

————. (2000) "Kant's Noninterventionalism and Recent Alternatives of Nonmilitary Intervention," pp. 149–159. In *Peacemaking: Lessons from the Past, Visions for the Future*. Edited by Judith Presler and Sally Scholz. Amsterdam: Rodopi.

————. (2002) "Diversity and Peace: Negative and Positive Forms," pp. 175–185. In *Community, Diversity, and Difference: Implications for Peace*. Edited by Alison Bailey and Paula J. Smithka. Amsterdam: Rodopi.

————. (2004) "Economic Democracy: The Final Frontier," pp. 121–136. In *Democracy and the Quest for Justice: Russian and American Perspectives*. Edited by William Gay and T. A. Alekseeva. Amsterdam: Rodopi.

————. (2006) "Apocalyptic Thinking versus Nonviolent Action: From Instilling Fear to Inspiring Hope," pp. 43–53. In *Spiritual and Political Dimensions of Nonviolence and Peace*. Edited by David Boersema and Katy Gray Brown. Amsterdam: Rodopi.

————. (2007a) "The New Reign of Terror: The Politics of Defining Weapons of Mass Destruction and Terrorism," pp.23–33. In *Philosophical Perspectives on the "War on Terrorism."* Edited by Gail Presbey. Amsterdam: Rodopi.

————. (2007b) "Supplanting Linguistic Violence," pp. 435–442. In *Gender Violence: Interdisciplinary Perspectives*. Second Edition. Edited by Laura L. O'Toole, Jessica R. Schiffman, and Margie L. Kiter Edwards. New York: New York University Press.

————. (2010) "Nonviolent Rhetoric in Geopolitics," pp. 31–37. In *Positive Peace: Reflections on Peace Education, Nonviolence and Social Change*. Edited by Andrew Fitz-Gibbon. Amsterdam: Rodopi.

Gortz, André. (1980) *Ecology as Politics*. Translated by Patsy Vigderman and Jonathan Clound. Boston, Mass.: South End Press.

Goulet, Denis. (1993) "Biological Diversity and Ethics Development," pp. 17–39. In *Ethics, Religion, and Biodiversity: Relations between Conservation and Cultural Values*. Edited by Lawrence S. Hamilton. Cambridge, UK: The While Horse Press.

Hall, David L. (1987) "Logos, Mythos, Chaos: Metaphysics as the Quest for Diversity," pp. 1_24. In *New Essays in Metaphysics*. Edited by Robert C. Neville. Albany: State University of New York Press.

Kant, Immanuel. (1983) *Perpetual Peace and Other Essays*. Translated by Ted Humphrey. Indianapolis, Ind.: Hackett.

Klare, Michael T. (1980) "Militarism: The Issues Today," pp. 26–46. In *Problems of Contemporary Militarism*. Edited by Asbjørn Eide and Marek Thee. New York: St. Martin's Press.

Lacy, William B. (1994) "Biodiversity, Cultural Diversity, and Food Equity," *Agriculture and Human Values*, 11:1 (Winter), pp. 3–9.

Lyell, Charles. (1997) *Principles of Geology*. London: Penguin.

Malthus, Thomas. (1914) *An Essay on Population*. New York: E. P. Denton & Co.

Outlaw, Lucius. (1992) "Against the Grain of Modernity: The Politics of Difference and the Conservation of 'Race,'" *Man and World*, 25, pp. 443–468.

Plato. (1941) *The Republic of Plato*. Translated by Francis MacDonald. Cornford, London: Oxford University Press.

Rawls, John. (1999) *A Theory of Justice*. Boston, Mass.: Belknap Press of Harvard University Press.

Rockefeller, Steven C. (1994) Comment, pp. 87–98. In Charles Taylor. *Multiculturalism: Examining the Politics of Recognition*. Edited by Amy Gutmann. Princeton, N.J.: Princeton University Press.

Russ, Joanna. (1983) *How to Suppress Women's Writing*. Austin: University of Texas Press.
Somerville, John. (1985) "Nuclear 'War' Is Omnicide," pp. 3–9. In *Nuclear War: Philosophical Perspectives*. Edited by Michael Allen Fox and Leo Groarke. New York: Peter Lang Publishing.
Weber, Max. (1968) *Economy and Society: An Outline of Interpretive Sociology*. Edited by Guenther Roth and Claus Wittich. Translated by Ephraim Fischoff. New York: Bedminster Press.
Wolff, Rober Paul, Barrington Moore, Jr., and Herbert Marcus. (1969) *A Critique of Pure Tolerance*. Boston, Mass.: Beacon Press.

Chapter Two
Wendy C. Hamblet

Benardette, Seth, David Grene, and Richard Lattimore, trans. (1960) *The Complete Greek Tragedies*. Volume 1. Chicago, Ill., University of Chicago.
Foucault, Michel. (1995) *Discipline and Punish: the Birth of the Prison*. Translated by Alan Sheridan. New York: Vintage Books.
———. (1997) Ethics: Subjectivity and Truth. Edited by Paul Rabinow. New York: The New York Press.
Hamblet, Wendy C. (2010) "Beyond Guilt and Mourning: A Critique of Postmodern Ethics," *Acorn* (Spring), Edited by Barry Gan.
Herrmann, Benedikt, Christian Thöni, and Simon Gätcher. (2008) "Antisocial Punishment Across Societies," *Science*, 319:5868, pp. 1362–1367.
Luther, Martin. (1957) *Luther's Ninety-Five Theses*. Philadelphia, Pa.: Fortress Press.
McGuire, James. (1999) *What Works: Reducing Reoffending*. Hoboken, N.J.: Wiley.
Rowling, Marjorie. (1979) *Life in Medieval Times*. New York: Paragon Books.
Rusche, Georg, and Otto Kirchheimer. (1939) *Punishment and Social Structure*. New York: Columbia University Press.
Sophocles. (2003) *Antigone*. Translated by David Franklin and John Harrison. Cambridge: Cambridge University Press.
Weber, Max. (2002) The Protestant Ethic and the Spirit of Capitalism. Edited and translated by Peter Baehr and Gordon C. Wells. New York: Penguin Books.

Chapter Three
Arnold L. Farr

Adorno, Theodor W. (2006) *History and Freedom*. Cambridge, Mass.: Polity Press.
———. (2005) *Minima Moralia*. New York: Verso.
———. (1987) *Negative Dialectics*. New York: Continuum.
Benjamin, Walter (1969) *Illuminations*. New York: Schocken Books.
Bernstein, J. M. (2001) *Adorno: Disenchantment and Ethics*. New York: Cambridge University Press.
Bourdieu, P. (1996) *Distinction: A Social Critique of the Judgment of Taste*. Cambridge, Mass.: Harvard University Press.
Farr, Arnold L. (2008) "Diversity, Color-Blindness, and Other Hegemonic Discourses," *Social Philosophy Today*, 24, pp. 91–105.
Gadamer, Hans-Georg (1988) *Truth and Method*. New York: Crossroad.

Horkheimer, Max, and Theodor W. Adorno. (1993) *Dialectic of Enlightenment*, New York: Continuum.

Kant, Immanuel. (2000) *The Metaphysics of Morals*. Cambridge, UK: Cambridge University Press.

Marcuse, Herbert (1965) "Repressive Tolerance." In *A Critique of Pure Tolerance*. Boston, Mass.: Beacon.

———. (1966) *One Dimensional Man*. Boston, Mass.: Beacon Press.

Marx, K. (2000) "The German Ideology" in *Karl Marx: Selected Writings*. New York: Oxford University Press.

Mills, Charles W. and Carole Pateman. (2007) *Contract and Domination*. Cambridge, Mass.: Polity.

Young, I. (2002) *Inclusion and Democracy*. New York: Oxford University Press.

Chapter Four
Andrew Fitz-Gibbon

Antonaccio, M. (2000) *Picturing the Human: The Moral Thought of Iris Murdoch*. Oxford: Oxford University Press.

Appiah, Kwame Anthony. (2006) *Cosmopolitanism: Ethics in a World of Strangers*. New York: W.W. Norton.

Arendt, Hannah, J. V. Scott, and J. C. Stark. (1996) *Love and Saint Augustine*. Chicago: The University of Chicago Press (original 1929).

Aristotle. (2004) *The Nicomachean Ethics*. Translated by James Alexander Kerr Thomson, Hugh Tredennick, and Jonathan Barnes. London: Penguin.

Black, Max. (1969) "The Gap Between 'Is' and 'Should,'" pp. 99–113. In Hudson, *The Is/Ought Question*.

Collins, Patricia Hill. (1990) *Black Feminist Thought: Knowledge, Consciousness, and the Politics of Empowerment*. New York: Routledge.

Crenshaw, Kimberlé Williams. (1991) "Mapping the Margins: Intersectionality, Identity Politics, and Violence Against Women of Color," *Stanford Law Review*, 43:6, pp. 1241–1299.

Davis, Angela Y. (1981) *Women, Race, and Class*. New York: Random House.

Fletcher, J. F. (1966) *Situation Ethics: The New Morality*. Philadelphia: Westminster.

Hudson, William Donald, ed. (1969) *The Is/Ought Question: A Collection of Papers on the Central Problem in Moral Philosophy*. Bristol: Macmillan.

Hume, David. (1969) *A Treatise on Human Nature*. London: Penguin (original 1739, 1740).

———. (2006). *An Enquiry Concerning the Principles of Morals*. Teddington, Greater London, UK: The Echo Library (original 1751).

Jagger, Alison M., and Paula S. Rothenberg, eds.. (1993) *Feminist Frameworks: Alternative Theoretical Accounts of the Relations between Men and Women*. New York: McGraw Hill.

James, Joy, ed. (1998) *The Angela Y. Davis Reader*. Malden, Mass.: Blackwell.

Kant, Immanuel. (1994) *Ethical Philosophy: The Complete Texts of Grounding for the Metaphysics of Morals and the Metaphysical Principles of Virtue, Part II of the Metaphysics of Morals*. Edited by James Wesley Wellington. Indianapolis, Ind.: Hackett (original, 1785, 1797).

Kierkegaard, Søren. (1962) *Works of Love: Kierkegaards's Writing, XVI.* Translated by H. V. Hong and E. H. Hong. Princeton, N. J.: Princeton University Press (original 1847).

Kourany, J. A., J. P. Sterba, and R. Tong. (1999) *Feminist Philosophies.* Upper Saddle River, N. J.: Prentice Hall.

MacIntyre, Alasdair. (1985) *After Virtue: A Study in Moral Theory.* London: Gerald Duckworth.

Moore, George Edward. (1988) *Principia Ethica.* Amherst, N. Y.: Prometheus Books.

Murdoch, Iris. (1970) *The Sovereignty of Good.* London: Routledge and Kegan Paul.

Rawls, John. (1971). *A Theory of Justice.* Cambridge, Mass.: Belknap Press of the Harvard University Press.

Roberts, Allan, and Doris Fisher. (1944) "You always hurt the ones you love." Decca Records, catalog number 18599.

Ruokonen, Floora. (2002) "Good, Self, and Unselfing—Reflections on Iris Murdoch's Moral Philosophy," *Austrian Ludwig Wittgenstein Society,* pp. 211–213.

Russell, Kathryn. (2007) "Feminist Dialectics and Marxist Theory," *Radical Philosophy Review,* 10:1, pp. 33–54.

Singer, Peter. (2000) *Writings on the Ethical Life.* New York: Harper Collins.

Chapter Five
Matthew Pianalto

Benjamin, M. (1990) *Splitting the Difference.* Lawrence: University of Kansas Press.

Brown, W. (2006). *Regulating Aversion: Tolerance in the Age of Identity and Empire.* Princeton, N.J.: Princeton University Press.

Calhoun, Cheshire (1995) "Standing for Something," *Journal of Philosophy,* 97:5, pp. 235–260.

Cowley, C. (2005) "Changing One's Mind about Moral Matters," *Ethical Theory and Practice,* 8:3, pp. 277–290.

Davion, V. (1991) "Integrity and Radical Change," pp. 180–192. In *Feminist Ethics.* Edited by C. Card. Lawrence: University of Kansas Press.

Frost, Robert. (1915) *North of Boston.* New York: Henry Holt & Co.

Gaita, R. (2000) *A Common Humanity.* London: Routledge.

Graham, P. (1998) "Saying 'No' to Compromise, 'Yes' to Integration," *Journal of Business Ethics,* 17, pp. 1007–1013.

Herman, B. (1996) "Pluralism and the Community of Moral Judgment," pp. 60–80. In *Tolerance: An Elusive Virtue.* Edited by D. Heyd. Princeton, N.J.: Princeton University Press.

King, Jr., Martin Luther. (1990) *A Testament of Hope: The Essential Writings and Speeches of Martin Luther King, Jr.* Ed. J. M. Washington. New York: Harper One

Lichtenberg, J. (1994) "Moral Certainty," *Philosophy,* 69:268, pp. 181–204.

Marcuse, Herbert (1969) "Repressive Tolerance," pp. 81–123. In *A Critique of Pure Tolerance.* Edited by R. P. Wolff, B. Moore, and H. Marcuse. Boston, Mass.: Beacon Press.

Oberdiek, Hans (2000) *Tolerance: Between Acceptance and Forbearance.* New York: Rowman and Littlefield.

Popper, Karl. (1987) "Toleration and Intellectual Responsibility," pp. 17–34. In *On Toleration.* Edited by S. Mendus and D. Edwards. Oxford: Clarendon Press.

Rawls, John. (2005) *Political Liberalism*. New York: Columbia University Press.
Taylor, G. (1981) "Integrity," *Proceedings of the Aristotelian Society*, Supplement 55, pp. 143–159.
Thoreau, Henry David. (2008) *Walden, Civil Disobedience, and Other Writings*. Edited by W. Rossi. New York: W. W. Norton & Co.
Warnock, Mary (1987) "The Limits of Toleration," pp. 123–139. In *On Toleration*. Edited by S. Mendus and D. Edwards. Oxford: Clarendon Press.
Williams, B. (1963) "A Critique of Utilitarianism," pp. 75–150. In *Utilitarianism: For and Against*. Edited by J. J. C. Smart and B. Williams. New York: Cambridge University Press.
Wolff, R. P., B. Moore, and Herbert Marcuse. (1969) *A Critique of Pure Tolerance*. Boston, Mass.: Beacon Press.

Chapter Six
V. Denise James

hooks, bell. (1995) *Killing Rage: Ending Racism*. New York: Holt and Company.
Jordan, June. (2002) *Some of Us Did Not Die: New and Selected Essays*. New York: Basic/Civitas Books.
Lorde, Audre. (1984) *Sister Outsider: Essays and Speeches*. Berkley: Crossing Press.
Miller, Jody. (2008) *Getting Played: African American Girls, Urban Inequality, and Violence*. New York: New York University Press.

Chapter Seven
Courtland Lewis

Drakulić, Slavenka. (1996) *Cafe Europa: Life After Communism*. New York: W. W. Norton & Company.
Havel, Václav. (1992) *Open Letters: Selected Writings, 1965–1990*. New York: Vintage.
Michnik, Adam. (1998) *Letters from Freedom: Post-Cold War Realities and Perspectives*. Berkeley: University of California Press.
Scarry, Elaine. (1985) *The Body in Pain: The Making and Unmaking of the World*. New York: Oxford University Press.
Volf, Miroslav. (2006) *The End of Memory: Remembering Rightly in a Violent World*. Grand Rapids, Mich.: William B. Eerdmans Publishing.
Wolfendale, Jessica. (2005) "The Hardened Heart: The Moral Dangers of Not Forgiving," *Journal of Social Philosophy*, 36:2, pp. 344–363.
Young, Iris Marion. (2006) "Responsibility and Global Justice: A Social Connection Model," *Social Philosophy and Policy*, 23:1, pp. 102–130.

Chapter Eight
Tanya Loughead

Alexander, Jacqui M. (2005) *Pedagogies of Crossing: Meditiations on Feminism, Sexual Politics, Memory, and the Sacred*. Durham, N.C.: Duke University Press.
Best, Steven, and Douglas Kellner. (1991) *Postmodern Theory: Critical Interrogations*. New York: Guilford Press.

————. (2002) "Postmodern Politics and the Battle for the Future," *Illuminations*. http://www.uta.edu/huma/illuminations/kell28.htm (accessed 01 October 2010).

————, eds. (1997) "Postmodern Theory: Critical Interrogations." In *The Postmodern Turn*. The Guilford Press, New York.

Caputo, John D. (2004) "Jacques Derrida (1930–2004)," *Journal for Cultural and Religious Theory*, 6:1 (December), pp. 6–9. http://www.jcrt.org/archives/06.1/caputo.pdf (accessed 01 October 2010).

Freud, Sigmund. (1961/1930) *Civilization and Its Discontents*. Translated by James Strachey. New York: W. W. Norton.

Freire, Paulo. (2000) *Pedagogy of the Oppressed*. New York: Continuum.

Hart, James G. (2008) "The Essential Look (*eidos*) of the Humanities: A Husserlian Phenomenology of the University," *Tijdschrift voor Filosofie*, 70, pp. 109–139.

Heidegger, Martin. (1962/1927) *Being and Time*. Translated by John Macquarrie and Edward Robinson. Oxford: Basil Blackwell.

Jameson, Fredric. (1991) *Postmodernism or the Cultural Logic of Late Capitalism*. Durham, N.C.: Duke University Press.

Kristeva, Julia. (2000/1996) The Sense and Non-Sense of Revolt: The Powers and Limits of Psychoanalysis. Translated by Jeanine Herman. New York: Columbia University Press.

————. (2002/1997) "What Revolt Today? Psychoanalysis and Freedom." In *Intimate Revolt: The Powers and Limits of Psychoanalysis*. Volume 2. Translated by Jeanine Herman. New York: Columbia University Press.

Marcuse, Herbert. (1978) *The Aesthetic Dimension: Toward a Critique of Marxist Aesthetics*. Translated by Herbert Marcuse and Erica Sherover. Boston, Mass.: Beacon Press.

Marcuse, Herbert. (1966/1955) *Eros and Civilization: A Philosophical Inquiry into Freud*. Boston, Mass.: Beacon Press.

Reitz, Charles. (2000) *Art, Alienation, and the Humanities: A Critical Engagement with Herbert Marcuse*. Albany: State University of New York Press.

Ricoeur, Paul. (1970/1965) *Freud and Philosophy: An Essay on Interpretation*. Translated by Denis Savage. New Haven, Conn.: Yale University Press.

ABOUT THE AUTHORS

ARNOLD L. FARR earned his PhD in philosophy in 1997 from the University of Kentucky. He was Associate Professor of Philosophy and Director of the Africana Studies Program at St. Joseph's University in Philadelphia, Pennsylvania, from 1996–2008. In 2008, Farr returned to the University of Kentucky as Associate Professor of Philosophy. His research includes German Idealism, Marxism, critical theory, and philosophy of race. He has published *Critical Theory and Democratic Vision: Herbert Marcuse and Recent Liberation Philosophies* (2009) and co-edited *Marginal Groups and Mainstream American Society* with A. Yolanda Estes, Patricia Smith, and Clelia Smyth (2000). He is currently working on a book titled *Misrecognition, Mimetic Rivalry, and One-Dimensionality: Toward a Critical Theory of Human Conflict and Social Pathologies*. In 2005, Farr founded the International Herbert Marcuse Society.

ANDREW FITZ-GIBBON is associate professor of philosophy and director of the Center for Ethics, Peace and Social Justice, at the State University of New York College at Cortland. He earned his PhD from the University of Newcastle-upon-Tyne, UK. His academic interests are in the areas of nonviolence, love, mysticism and community. He is the author or co-author of six books and fourteen articles and book chapters in peer reviewed volumes. His latest book, *Positive Peace*, was published in spring 2010, and he is working on a book titled *Love as a Guide to Morals*. Andrew is Editor of the special series, Social Philosophy Series (Rodopi, VIBS). He is a fellow of the American Philosophical Practitioners Association, certified in client counseling. Also, Andrew is abbot of the Lindisfarne Community, Ithaca NY, a small ecumenical religious order.

WILLIAM C. GAY is Professor of Philosophy at the University of North Carolina at Charlotte. He is past editor of *Concerned Philosophers for Peace Newsletter* (1987–2002) and, since 2002, Editor of CPP's Special Series on "Philosophy of Peace" (Rodopi, VIBS). He is past President and past Executive Director of Concerned Philosophers for Peace. With T. A. Alekseeva, he is coauthor of *Capitalism with a Human Face: The Quest for a Middle Road in Russian Politics* (Rowman and Littlefield, 1996); and coeditor of *On the Eve of the 21st Century: Perspectives of Russian and American Philosophers* (Rowman and Littlefield, 1994), and *Democracy and the Quest for Justice: Russian and American Perspectives* (Rodopi, 2004). With Michael Pearson, he is coauthor of *The Nuclear Arms Race* (American Library Association, 1987). With I. I. Mazour and A. N. Chumakov, he is coeditor of *Global Studies Encyclopedia* (Raduga, 2003). He has also published articles and book chapters on peace, justice, and nonviolence from the perspectives of philosophy of language and political philosophy.

WENDY C. HAMBLET is a Canadian philosopher who serves as Associate Professor of Liberal Studies at North Carolina A&T State University. She is also Director of Therapeia Ethics Consulting, a firm that offers professional development applications of Organizational Ethics tailored for government and business settings. Hamblet is the author of a number of books exploring the phenomenology of violence, the latest of which include *Savage Constructions: The Myth of African Savagery and Punishment* (2008); and *Shame: A Philosophical Study* (2011).

V. DENISE JAMES, who took the PhD in philosophy from Emory University in Atlanta, Georgia, is currently Assistant Professor of Philosophy at University of Dayton, Ohio. She is a black feminist philosopher whose interests include contemporary American social and political thought, pragmatism, and the philosophy of geography. Her current work is concerned with bridging the divide between radical, transformative political theory and local democratic practices.

COURTLAND LEWIS is a PhD candidate at the University of Tennessee, where he studies Social/Political philosophy and Ethics. His primary interests in these areas include the examination of the role of justice and dignity in fostering responsibility and forgiveness after mass atrocities and genocide. Other research interests include the study of popular culture and philosophy. Lewis is also involved in many community projects.

TANYA LOUGHEAD is an Assistant Professor in the Department of Philosophy at Canisius College, a Jesuit liberal arts college in Buffalo, New York. She completed her Masters and PhD degrees at the Catholic University of Leuven in Belgium. At Canisius College, Dr. Loughead co-founded and runs programs on Ethics and Justice, and is working to establish an Institute for Ethics and Justice. She specializes in the area of Contemporary Continental Philosophy and is interested in scholarship and teaching on justice. Loughead has published articles on the works of Maurice Blanchot, Emmanuel Lévinas, Simone Weil, Jacques Derrida, and Jean-Luc Marion, among others. Her recent work is concerned with the purpose of the university in late capitalism.

MATTHEW PIANALTO is an Assistant Professor of Philosophy at Eastern Kentucky University. He has published articles on various topics in ethical theory and value theory, such as moral conflict, well-being, and the application of Wittgenstein's ideas to ethics. His main philosophical interests center on problems of moral disagreement and understanding, the relationships among experience, expression, and judgment, and practical issues concerning the environment and animals. With Edward Minar, he co-edited the Spring 2010 issue of *Philosophical Topics*, on topics in ethics.

DANIELLE POE is an Associate Professor of Philosophy at the University of Dayton. Her research interests include contemporary issues of peace and the work of Luce Irigary. Her recent work includes, "Woman Mother, and Non-violent Activisim" in *Positive Peace: Reflections on Peace Education* (2010); "Donut Shops and World Peace: Subsidiarity and the Biasfor the Local," *Jounal of Globalization Studies* (2010); and "Mothers and Civil Disobe-dience," *Peace and Justice Studies* (Summer 2009). Poe aslo co-edited *Parceling the Globe: Philosophical Explorations in Globalization, Global Behavior, and Peace* (with Eddy Souffrant, 2008).

INDEX

engagement, *con't.*
  tolerant e., 46–51,
  victims/wrongdoers, e. between, 68
enlightenment, 25, 29, 33
  e. ideals, 12–14
  e. thinkers, 24
entitlements, gender, 59
environmentalism, 6, 7
envy, 21
epoché. See bracketing
equality, 25–28, 31, 32, 36, 54
eros, 39
Eros and Civilization (Marcuse), 74
erosic love, 39, 40
"The Essential Look (*eidos*) of the Humanities" (Hart), 76
ethical conditioning, 19
ethnicity, 7, 36
ethnocentrism, 7
Europe, 14–17, 19, 31
evil, 57
  man's e. nature, 18
  penal e., 9
evolution, 3, 13
executioner, 13
exploitation, 5, 24

face-to-face meetings, 63
fear, 6, 31, 53, 70
  rage, f. of articulating, 56–58
  rape and f., 61
  resistance to oppression, f. cripples, 60
federalism, 8
feminis(m)(ts), 80, 82
  black f., 36, 53, 54, 56
  f. philosophers, 29
  white f., 36, 57, 58
Fletcher, Joseph, 39
food, 14, 28
Foucault, Michel, 11–14, 17–19, 78
Frederick II, 16
freedom, 23, 25, 53, 56
  buying f. from God's punishment, 16
  engage, f. to, 73
  fear, f. from, 31
  re-birth, f. as, 77

Soviet communism and f., 6
  spontaneous f., 20
Freire, Paulo, 77, 80
French Revolution, 13, 74
Freud, Sigmund, 74, 79, 81
  Civilization and Its Discontents, 79
friendship, 39, 40
Fukuyama, Francis, 8

Gadamer, Hans-Georg, 24, 25
  Truth and Method, 24
Gallie, Walter Bryce, 7
Galtung, Johan, 6
Gandhi, Mahatma, 67
Gätcher, Simon, 18
gays, 25
gender, 7, 24, 36, 37
  g.-based violations, 54–61
  g. entitlements, 59
  race and g. intersection, 58
genocide, 6
geo-political relations, 3
"The German Ideology" (Marx), 24
Getting Played (Miller), 54, 55, 58
goals, 6, 19, 21, 58, 73–75
Gorgias (Plato), 10, 20
Gorz, André, 5, 6
Goulet, Denis, 4
grants, 10, 76
greed, 17, 21, 34
guilt, 20, 68, 69
gypsies, 14, 68

habitus, 25, 26
Hall, David, 4, 5
happiness, 39
harassment, 53–57, 59, 60
Hart, James G., 76, 77, 90
  "The Essential Look (*eidos*) of the Humanities," 76
hatred, 21, 57, 58, 65, 66
Havel, Václav, 70, 71
healing, 64–66, 68, 71, 80
  political h., 63
  h. rage, 54
  h. therapies, 13

VIBS

The **Value Inquiry Book Series** is co-sponsored by:

Titles Published

Volumes 1 - 194 see www.rodopi.nl

195. Josef Šmajs, *Evolutionary Ontology: Reclaiming the Value of Nature by Transforming Culture*. A volume in **Central-European Value Studies**

196. Giuseppe Vicari, *Beyond Conceptual Dualism: Ontology of Consciousness, Mental Causation, and Holism in John R. Searle's Philosophy of Mind*. A volume in **Cognitive Science**

197. Avi Sagi, *Tradition vs. Traditionalism: Contemporary Perspectives in Jewish Thought*. Translated from Hebrew by Batya Stein. A volume in **Philosophy and Religion**

198. Randall E. Osborne and Paul Kriese, Editors, *Global Community: Global Security*. A volume in **Studies in Jurisprudence**

199. Craig Clifford, *Learned Ignorance in the Medicine Bow Mountains: A Reflection on Intellectual Prejudice*. A volume in **Lived Values: Valued Lives**

200. Mark Letteri, *Heidegger and the Question of Psychology: Zollikon and Beyond*. A volume in **Philosophy and Psychology**

201. Carmen R. Lugo-Lugo and Mary K. Bloodsworth-Lugo, Editors, *A New Kind of Containment: "The War on Terror," Race, and Sexuality*. A volume in **Philosophy of Peace**

202. Amihud Gilead, *Necessity and Truthful Fictions: Panenmentalist Observations*. A volume in **Philosophy and Psychology**

203. Fernand Vial, *The Unconscious in Philosophy, and French and European Literature: Nineteenth and Early Twentieth Century*. A volume in **Philosophy and Psychology**

204. Adam C. Scarfe, Editor, *The Adventure of Education: Process Philosophers on Learning, Teaching, and Research*. A volume in **Philosophy of Education**

205. King-Tak Ip, Editor, *Environmental Ethics: Intercultural Perspectives*. A volume in **Studies in Applied Ethics**

206. Evgenia Cherkasova, *Dostoevsky and Kant: Dialogues on Ethics.* A volume in **Social Philosophy**

207. Alexander Kremer and John Ryder, Editors, *Self and Society: Central European Pragmatist Forum*, Volume Four. A volume in **Central European Value Studies**

208. Terence O'Connell, *Dialogue on Grief and Consolation*. A volume in **Lived Values, Valued Lives**

209. Craig Hanson, *Thinking about Addiction: Hyperbolic Discounting and Responsible Agency*. A volume in **Social Philosophy**

210. Gary G. Gallopin, *Beyond Perestroika: Axiology and the New Russian Entrepreneurs*. A volume in **Hartman Institute Axiology Studies**

211. Tuija Takala, Peter Herissone-Kelly, and Søren Holm, Editors, *Cutting Through the Surface: Philosophical Approaches to Bioethics*. A volume in **Values in Bioethics**

212. Neena Schwartz: *A Lab of My Own*. A volume in **Lived Values, Valued Lives**

213. Krzysztof Piotr Skowroński, *Values and Powers: Re-reading the Philosophical Tradition of American Pragmatism*. A volume in **Central European Value Studies**

214. Matti Häyry, Tuija Takala, Peter Herissone-Kelly and Gardar Árnason, Editors, *Arguments and Analysis in Bioethics*. A volume in **Values in Bioethics**

215. Anders Nordgren, *For Our Children: The Ethics of Animal Experimentation in the Age of Genetic Engineering*. A volume in **Values in Bioethics**

216. James R. Watson, Editor, *Metacide: In the Pursuit of Excellence*. A volume in **Holocaust and Genocide Studies**

217. Andrew Fitz-Gibbon, Editor, *Positive Peace: Reflections on Peace Education, Nonviolence, and Social Change*. A volume in **Philosophy of Peace**

218. Christopher Berry Gray, *The Methodology of Maurice Hauriou: Legal, Sociological, Philosophical.* A volume in **Studies in Jurisprudence**

219. Mary K. Bloodsworth-Lugo and Carmen R. Lugo-Lugo, *Containing (Un)American Bodies: Race, Sexuality, and Post-9/11 Constructions of Citizenship.* A volume in **Philosophy of Peace**

220. Roland Faber, Brian G. Henning, Clinton Combs, Editors, *Beyond Metaphysics? Explorations in Alfred North Whitehead's Late Thought.* A volume in **Contemporary Whitehead Studies**

221. John G. McGraw, *Intimacy and Isolation (Intimacy and Aloneness: A Multi-Volume Study in Philosophical Psychology, Volume One)*, A volume in **Philosophy and Psychology**

222. Janice L. Schultz-Aldrich, Introduction and Edition, "*Truth" is a Divine Name, Hitherto Unpublished Papers of Edward A. Synan, 1918-1997.* A volume in **Gilson Studies**

223. Larry A. Hickman, Matthew Caleb Flamm, Krzysztof Piotr Skowroński and Jennifer A. Rea, Editors, *The Continuing Relevance of John Dewey: Reflections on Aesthetics, Morality, Science, and Society.* A volume in **Central European Value Studies**

224. Hugh P. McDonald, *Creative Actualization: A Meliorist Theory of Values.* A volume in **Studies in Pragmatism and Values**

225. Rob Gildert and Dennis Rothermel, Editors, *Remembrance and Reconciliation.* A volume in **Philosophy of Peace**

226. Leonidas Donskis, Editor, *Niccolò Machiavelli: History, Power, and Virtue.* A volume in **Philosophy, Literature, and Politics**

227. Sanya Osha, *Postethnophilosophy.* A volume in **Social Philosophy**

228. Rosa M. Calcaterra, Editor, *New Perspectives on Pragmatism and Analytic Philosophy.* A volume in **Studies in Pragmatism and Values**

229. Danielle Poe, Editor, *Communities of Peace: Confronting Injustice and Creating Justice.* A volume in **Philosophy of Peace**

www.ingramcontent.com/pod-product-compliance
Lightning Source LLC
Chambersburg PA
CBHW050536270326
41926CB00015B/3260